Praise for *Remember Who You Are*

Here's a beautiful reminder that success is not measured by dollars but by the fulfillment of personal priorities. Feeling connected and supported may provide more value than a promotion that depletes energy and alienates those you care about most. This book will help you take a deep breath and advance in ways that will allow you to live fully, love deeply and leave a legacy.

Dan Miller, *New York Times bestselling author,*
48 Days to the Work You Love

Remember Who You Are provides a transparent look at the journeys Paula and Lisa took — from entry level positions using their STEM backgrounds to C-suite positions with global responsibilities. Companies benefit from bold, authentic, diverse leadership. This book gives sound advice to our next generation of female talent aiming to succeed in this industry.

Jim Goodnight, *SAS CEO*

Paula and Lisa share enlightening leadership and success insights — leveraging their UNC Chapel Hill public health and pharmacy degrees as launching pads to achieving executive status around the world. No matter where a woman is on her life's journey and what professional goals she is pursuing, *Remember Who You Are* can motivate and guide in good times and through challenging moments.

Chancellor Carol L. Folt, *The University of North Carolina at Chapel Hill*

Remember Who You Are is a terrific must-read for career women (and men). Paula and Lisa share personal insights into how they have balanced work and family as they moved into the corporate boardroom. They show how to "keep your cool" when trying to nail ...
forces and deal with competitors, all wh
home front. I loved this book!

Karna Small Bodman, *Former White H*
Winning Author

We need one another. As female executives, we are better together. In *Remember Who You Are*, Paula and Lisa beautifully describe practical ways for you to achieve success, create balance and experience fulfillment. Life can be hard. Remembering who you are will provide an anchor for your soul during challenging times. This delightful book will have you turning the page quickly with great anticipation for what's to come next. Get ready to be empowered and encouraged like never before.

Dr. Jevonnah "Lady J" Ellison, *Certified Leading Business Coach, Speaker & Author, Forbes Coaches Council*

As a father of a daughter who is in the early stages of her professional career, finding the right words to motivate and guide her can be a challenge. *Remember Who You Are* sums it up perfectly. Paula and Lisa have developed a creative way to convey their experiences, as well as the experiences of fellow female colleagues in this insightful and thought-provoking read. Their words are empowering, encouraging and honest, making you want to absorb everything on the page. Whether you're a woman, or man, looking to jumpstart your career or take it to the next level, I highly recommend reading this book.

Doug Lane, *President & CEO, Capgemini Government Solutions*

Filled with timely — and timeless — insights and counsel, *Remember Who You Are* is like having multiple mentors in your pocket. Make notes, highlight passages, and reference it again and again. You likely will take away something different yet equally meaningful each time.

Valerie A. Jackson, J.D., *Senior Advisor to the Management Committee and Firmwide Director of Diversity & Inclusion, K&L Gates*

An open and honest window into the careers and personal lives of two highly successful female executives, Paula and Lisa reflectively share how they achieved "C-level" success and fulfillment while fighting for and maintaining a healthy sense of balance. Woven together through their own real-life stories and engaging style, their insights are well founded and motivating. A fantastic read full of practical wisdom for anyone navigating a career and life, I am looking forward to sharing with my two daughters!

James P. Cain, *U.S. Ambassador (Ret.); Cain Global Partners, LLC*

Lisa and Paula have teamed up for engaging and practical advice for any woman seeking the ever-elusive balance in their lives. What a great read you will find inspiring and relatable! They share their struggles, triumphs, and paths to success with examples of real experiences I find fascinating and exceedingly helpful.

Debra Morgan, *WRAL-TV Anchor/Reporter*

Remember Who You Are is a thought provoking book for anyone interested in achieving professional and personal success without sacrificing one for the other. Paula and Lisa provide engaging stories and practical advise to anyone caught up in the inner work/life conundrum. These strong and successful women lived it. Now they're transparently sharing their key lessons learned with the world.

Myron J Radio, *Author, Executive Coach, Strategy Execution Consultant*

Through their own stories as business executives and those of the women they've coached, Paula and Lisa provide real advice that works — on how we, as women, can stop competing with each other and start complementing and supporting each other. *Remember Who You Are* is an excellent read for all working women.

Diana Faison, *Partner, Flynn Heath Holt*

REMEMBER

Who YOU Are

Achieve Success. Create Balance. Experience Fulfillment.

REMEMBER
Who
YOU
Are

Achieve Success.
Create Balance.
Experience Fulfillment.

PAULA BROWN STAFFORD
& LISA T. GRIMES

NEW YORK

LONDON • NASHVILLE • MELBOURNE • VANCOUVER

Remember Who You Are

Achieve Success. Create Balance. Experience Fulfillment.

The forewords in this book and the letters that are quoted at the ends of chapters are used with permission.

The stories and examples used in this book are based upon actual experiences. Names, situations and identifying facts have been altered or generalized and any resemblance to specific individuals is unintentional.

Published in New York, New York, by Morgan James Publishing. Morgan James is a trademark of Morgan James, LLC. www.MorganJamesPublishing.com

The Morgan James Speakers Group can bring authors to your live event. For more information or to book an event visit The Morgan James Speakers Group at www.TheMorganJamesSpeakersGroup.com.

ISBN 9781683506478 paperback
ISBN 9781683506485 eBook
Library of Congress Control Number: 2017909906

Cover Design by: Rachel Lopez

Interior Design by: Paul Curtis

In an effort to support local communities, raise awareness and funds, Morgan James Publishing donates a percentage of all book sales for the life of each book to Habitat for Humanity Peninsula and Greater Williamsburg.

Get involved today! Visit
www.MorganJamesBuilds.com

Dedication

To our husbands, Greg and Ed,
and our children, Celia, Jackson, Collin and Eric

Contents

Foreword (Her Perspective)

When Paula Brown Stafford approached me about writing a foreword for the book that she and Lisa Grimes were working on, I jumped at the opportunity. I was thrilled to learn that she and Lisa were writing a guide for professional women — to help them achieve success in the workplace while maintaining balance and fulfillment in their personal lives.

As most professionals — both female and male — can attest, balancing a demanding work life with a happy home and personal life can seem incredibly difficult at times. In fact, throughout my professional career at AT&T, Fidelity Investments, Harvard Business School, and now with the American Red Cross, I've experienced many of the frustrations and missteps that go hand in hand with our notions of trying to have and do it all. As a result, I am an enthusiastic proponent of anything that will help the next generation of female professionals avoid making the mistakes that I made.

When I read the initial manuscript that Paula and Lisa put together, I found the life events and lessons they detailed to be eminently relatable with my own experiences as a female executive in the corporate, academic, and now non-profit worlds. On a personal level, what immediately resonated with me was their call for professional women to take the time and effort to help other women in the workplace. Forming relationships and lasting bonds with female colleagues has been an instrumental part of my professional life — whether it be through more structured mentoring relationships, informal networking opportunities, or even a coffee session to vent and exchange workplace tips.

When I was promoted to a senior executive role at AT&T, I was one of only seven female senior leaders in the entire organization. When I left AT&T in 1998, 20 percent of the officers were female. To this day, one of my proudest professional accomplishments is knowing that I forged relationships with nearly all of these remarkable women. We shared advice — not only on such things as career advancement and the work culture at AT&T, but also on such topics as managing a successful work-life balance and juggling continuing education opportunities with our demanding work schedules. While I did serve as a formal mentor for a number of these wonderful women, I realize now that I learned just as much from them as I hope they did from me.

These days, I often tell people that I have the very best job in the world. Working at the American Red Cross, I get to experience both the amazing resilience and the tremendous generosity of the American people. In fact, when I reflect on the arc of my career, I feel truly fortunate to have enjoyed so many different professional opportunities and challenges, and to have learned a great deal along the way. Yet there is still so much I wish I could tell a younger version of myself to help her out along her professional journey.

First and foremost, I would tell this younger version of me that life will throw you a lot of curveballs. In fact, I've found that things hardly ever go according to the perfect plan you envisioned for yourself. As a young professional, I had no idea I would deal with such obstacles as getting divorced, or not being able to get pregnant with the love of my life (my wonderful second husband of 34 years, Don), or being diagnosed with breast cancer twice. Life truly is an off-road adventure – and you have to adjust, be flexible and pick yourself back up when things don't go your way. If you do, great things will come from what you may initially view as a disappointment.

Another thing I would tell my younger self is that you can't be perfect at everything. When you're juggling a busy work schedule with your personal life and your obligations to family and friends, you have to come to grips with the fact that there won't always be time to keep your house impeccably clean or to put together the perfect dinner party for your neighbors. Along these same lines, it's important that you have 'low-maintenance' friends who understand this — and who won't make you feel guilty when you can't call them back right away, or when you serve them delivery pizza instead of a gourmet meal.

And a final piece of advice I would tell the younger version of myself: Be present where you are. When you're in a work meeting, give that meeting, and the people in it, your full attention. But when you're out and about with friends, or spending quality time with loved ones at home, be sure to give them your total focus. Of course, this is getting harder and harder to do these days given the omnipresence of mobile devices. But if you can be present where you are, you'll enjoy life more and you'll also achieve better results in whatever you're doing.

So for all the professional women who are reading these words — and professional men too, for that matter — I hope you'll continue reading this book. I think you'll find the lessons and advice that Paula and Lisa share to be applicable to your own life in a number of ways

— whether you're a newly hired college grad or a seasoned manager. Avoiding the mistakes others have made is certainly better than making those same missteps yourself. This book gives you an opportunity to learn from two highly respected, personable and caring business leaders as you move forward on your path to professional success and personal fulfillment.

Gail McGovern
President and CEO
American Red Cross

Foreword (His Perspective)

When Paula and Lisa asked me to write a foreword from a man's perspective for *Remember Who You Are,* I eagerly agreed — not only because I believe in their mission of helping women navigate their careers meaningfully and successfully, but also because I've learned a few things in my years of leading businesses that I want to share.

I look back and see how I have evolved from some mix of unaware biases and sheer ignorance to someone who is far more conscious of the power of words, and actions, and culture. But there are some who have not moved an inch in their outdated thinking, which is why we need books like this to empower women — and to educate men.

First, a mea culpa. I am guilty of stereotypes. I once boarded a plane where I was introduced to the pilot and the captain, one a man and the other a woman. My first inclination was to assume that the man was the higher-ranking captain. I don't know where that assumption came from, but fortunately, I silently challenged my thinking. Within minutes I learned that the woman was the captain. The question I asked then, and continue to ask, is: *Why did I assume that the man was the captain?* Indeed, where do these insidious assumptions come from?

I have had some other moments that I am not proud of. I remember being at a dinner where a female executive VP and her subordinate male CIO of a prominent company joined me. The CIO loved soccer, as do I. Before I knew it, we were off in an intense conversation about soccer stars, international teams, and predictions of who would reign supreme.

I suddenly noticed that the executive VP had no awareness of soccer and was probably feeling on the outside looking in. Now there was a time in my life where I might not have noticed this, but since I did, I was able to subtly move the conversation to a topic that engaged us all.

This moment spurred more questions for me: *How did we so quickly land on sports (often, but not always, a male-dominated topic)? What should we do when common passions hijack a conversation that excludes others?* And finally: *Is there something that she could have done to engage in the conversation? Was domain expertise — in this case, soccer — essential to join in?* If you are that person who can find a toehold in unknown territory, and somehow join in, it helps. Not everyone can, but the best bridges result when they're built from both directions.

Now I began my foreword by claiming that I have evolved from some early and faulty assumptions about men and women. I believe this because I remember my teaching moments. One came when I was working at Lotus, a major high-tech company back in the early 1980s and 1990s.

I was in a meeting at 5:30 p.m. one day when I noticed that one woman kept glancing at her watch, and I stupidly asked, "Calendar check?" Her response was, "No, but if I could be excused to call my husband, I'll be fine." I asked whether anyone else had an issue, and when one woman said, "Yes, day care," I asked if there was anyone else.

Four hands went up — four women with responsibilities, all feeling the stress and pressure and guilt. I had been unaware.

Shortly after, we decided the group would never again meet at the end of the day. A new awareness yielded a new behavior — one of many to come.

My wife and I have a son and two daughters, and I have come to realize that women's challenges do not begin when they enter the workplace; they begin in childhood. Creating an environment where they are confident, feel empowered and see no boundaries sets the stage for everything they do. We never wanted to make our daughters feel as if they couldn't do anything a boy/man could do, whether it was sports, business or any profession. They are now very successful businesswomen but were shocked when they entered a world where they faced sexism once a week or more.

I share these stories, hoping that I don't seem boorish, to admit that I have had to reframe the way I view gender roles. As a CEO, I had ascribed to the importance of setting people up for success, but I don't think that I fully understood what that meant. I did not see some of the hidden obstacles that can sabotage success, whether they are stereotypes that we unconsciously hold, or social interactions that inadvertently exclude, or work schedules that assume 24/7 availability, or family responsibilities we presume are not equally shared (I call that my "Lotus moment").

I am happy to contribute to this book because I understand its importance, for both men and women. We need to build an awareness of the pernicious yet subtle threats that challenge women who are trying to succeed. This year we've read about companies that have occupied the hall of shame when it comes to sexism in the workplace. Who will be next? Only by building awareness will senior managers, most of whom today are men, stand up with a "no tolerance" policy.

I am proud that *Remember Who You Are* gives us a language and a way to address gender inequity. New challenges await, so the conversation will need to be ongoing, with new content and new models. In our brave new world, for example, we must be equipped to handle cyber harassment. In a global economy we must understand the challenges of extending our values to countries with more paternalistic traditions. There are so many ways for us to fail, but failure is not an option.

In the end, all successful efforts begin with building awareness. From there, bridges can be built. These bridges allow those who haven't yet moved an inch to suddenly move that inch, and then maybe two. The process will have started. Persistence will have paid off as we find and internalize our own "Lotus moments."

Robert K. Weiler
Executive Vice President, Global Business Units
Oracle

The Missing Piece

"I'm having a crisis. Do you have a few minutes?" reads an urgent text from a female business owner struggling with a decision that just didn't feel right in her gut.

"My (female) boss is making me miserable. I don't know what to do or how to get out of it," laments a 30-year-old lawyer in Manhattan.

"Should I go for that promotion, leave the company or just accept things and stay where I am?" asks a young professional.

"I'm not sure the best way to tell management I don't want to go back to work full time right after I have the baby," worries a working career mom.

"Yes, you get it … finally," sighs a C-suite executive who spends so much time managing her team and her family there is no time left for personal relationships that fulfill *her*. No one to "get" *her*.

Every day we hear from women like this. Women like you. Women in business who long for … what? Success in business, work/

life balance, a feeling of personal fulfillment? Yes, these are important and noble goals, and we will help you achieve them. But while you are busy managing others, being managed, or dealing with the impossible demands of trying to be everything to everyone at home and at work, we suspect there is something deeper that is missing.

Time and time again, we have found the real missing piece is the connection — specifically, the connection with other women. Women like you — smart, goal-oriented, trying to do and have it all — are often left feeling disconnected, unsupported, not enough, never enough. We hear it in your voices, see it in your faces — a longing to feel connected. As working moms, we feel it too. We wished for female mentors when we were navigating our careers and juggling the demands of family life. Someone who could listen and guide us. Someone who could validate our feelings, give us the courage to act, or even talk us off the ledge, when necessary. Our mentors (each other) came later in life, but it doesn't have to be that way for you.

The best news is — and we are so excited to share it — it is within our power to help *find* and *be* the connections that will empower, support and complement. It's not just about breaking glass ceilings; it's not about competing for that *one* female board position. It's about swinging open doors and throwing open windows so more women can walk through, take in the view from the next floor, or take a risk and veer off the paved path in search of something new. And doing it knowing another woman has her back, instead of worrying about someone stabbing her in the back. The success will follow.

Our Story

The two of us weren't enemies, but we certainly weren't friends. You could call us fierce competitors. As the vice presidents of the sales divisions for two of the largest clinical research organizations in the pharmaceutical industry, we knew "of" each other before we actually knew each other. It was not uncommon for us to see each other at trade shows or pass each other in a client's lobby as we were each vying for a multimillion-dollar contract, knowing only one of our teams would walk away with the deal. Our secret thoughts of each other? Paula recalls Lisa's striking presence and her no-nonsense approach … the "whole package." Lisa recalls Paula as smart, capable, someone she didn't want to battle head-to-head.

After many years, curiosity got the better of us, and a networking lunch launched a friendship as we both realized that *complementing each other was much better than competing*. We found in each other a perfect sounding board. We are both working mothers and wives. We have bought and sold companies. Each of us worked her way up from entry level to be named someone's Woman of the Year, yet we still struggle with keeping up with the paperwork and curveballs of life.

Do you know how refreshing it is to meet an authentic woman? A woman who gets frustrated, a woman who stumbles? A woman who is willing to say to herself: *It is OK not to do it all and have it all, so can you please stop trying?* That is the connection we found with each other and want to share with you. We are about to get real with the challenges we have encountered while trying to achieve success, create balance, and experience fulfillment. We made some mistakes and could have handled some situations better. We'll tell you all about it. The guilt over leaving your husband and baby for a business trip only to have a hurricane hit while you are gone? That's real. The feeling of failure when you have to lay off employees and shut the company doors? That's real.

But we'll also show you what worked for us and challenge you to develop your own personal brand, guided by your priorities. Once you do this, everything else will become easier to manage. Having your own brand is like having a road map you can refer to when you reach a fork in the road.

If you find yourself swamped in meetings but not feeling effective, we get that too. Men in boardrooms routinely comment that women apologize too much or talk in upspeak (ending your sentences like questions) in meetings. Both undermine your confidence and make you appear insecure. Or maybe you go too far in the other direction and come on so strong you are viewed as defensive and aggressive. We have been those women.

Today we combine our strengths, bolster each other in our weaknesses and share our experiences with younger female professionals. But still, we don't know it all. That is why we have asked nine of our powerhouse peers to write letters, independent of one another, to their younger selves about what they wish they had known earlier in their careers. At the end of each chapter you will find these letters. Letters from women in different industries and from different parts of the globe, and yet in many ways more alike than they are different. They have all reached the top levels in their careers, but have also struggled with the same challenges and fears you have. If hindsight is 20/20, you will reap the benefits of their insights. We are grateful they are willing to share their stories, which we hope help you avoid common pitfalls.

In taking the time to write one of these letters, one executive told us, "Thank you for the gift you just gave me." Viewing the opportunity to convey her personal thoughts as a gift is a testament to the fact that we all have a need to connect with, and a desire to help, one another. As we share stories and encouragement in these pages, we hope you will be inspired to give back by sharing your gifts and stories and to always *Remember Who You Are.*

Part One

Achieve Success

"Somehow, you have to make a commitment to get better every day, no matter how successful you were the day before."
~ Pat Summitt

1

Building Your Brand

"The grand essentials to happiness in this life are something to do, something to love, and something to hope for."
~ Joseph Addison

by Paula

"Remember who you are!" my parents would call after me as I hurried off the porch of our modest brick ranch home nestled on a hilltop on the outskirts of Raleigh. As a teenager heading out on a date or with friends, I may have rolled my eyes, but I knew what they meant. They were challenging me to remember what they had taught me, the values they had instilled in me … and to behave. They wanted me to stay true

to myself and not go out and try to be somebody else, especially if it was to impress others. At the time, I had no idea what a touchstone that phrase would become for me as I was building my career.

Growing up in North Carolina, I came from a family of workers. My grandfather, with no education to speak of, was a cook in the Navy. When he came back to Raleigh, he did the only thing that made sense — he opened a restaurant and worked his butt off. Baxley's Family Restaurant became an institution in Raleigh, and it was a family affair. At 10 years old, I was cleaning tables. At 13, I was a time-card-punching waitress making my own money. There were no silver spoons. Just honest, hard work and high expectations. There was pride, and there was satisfaction in a job well done.

Fast forward to my late thirties: While I was attending a weeklong program at the Center for Creative Leadership in Greensboro, North Carolina, my parents' words, *"Remember who you are,"* came back to me when the instructor asked, *"What is your personal brand?"* In other words, *"Who are you?"*

My first reaction was a dumbfounded look. *"What brand? Why do I need a brand?"*

Well, your personal brand is the core of who you are, not unlike your company's corporate values. It is also your reputation. It is what you project to the outside world and probably dictates a lot about where and how you will fit at a particular company. People's opinions and expectations of you will be defined by what kind of person they believe you to be. YOU need to determine and build your own unique brand instead of letting other people build it for you. Once you do that, you will develop consistency, and people will realize who you are through your words and actions. It can become the filter through which you live your life and can overflow into everything from your personal management style to your relationships at home. It's worth investing in.

Be Intentional

So how do you find, define, and share your brand? You do it intentionally because you will live with it for a very long time. And you don't want to rebrand yourself later — that would be tough and confusing to others.

To find your brand you might go through a little exercise. Talk to a few trusted people whose opinions you value. People you know will be honest with you. Ask them what words they would use to describe you. Ask yourself the same. And not just how you would describe yourself at this moment, but who you want to be. It is possible to build the best version of yourself and still remain true to who you are. *What do you want people to think of when they hear your name?*

Self-reflection can be daunting and uncomfortable, but it can be cleansing and yield amazing results. Don't be afraid to lay it all out there. Look for others, both inside and outside the workplace, you would like to emulate. And Google. If you are looking for answers it's hard to beat a good Google search. We don't mean create a fictional version of yourself, but there are a lot of wise folks out there who have valuable stories and lessons to share. Something will resonate with you. In fact, you probably will begin to see a pattern of something that speaks to you. Be mindful.

For me, it took months of searching, reflecting, and thinking about my roots to make sure I was being absolutely true to who I am and not just what others want me to be or what I think others want me to be. But I discovered my unique personal brand. I am authentic, discerning, a server to others (note: server not servant), and a solutions provider. I am passionate about sharing my brand with others, and I strive to have my words and actions convey that brand consistently at work and at home.

Another interesting exercise that helped me crystallize my brand came at another leadership conference just a few years ago. We were asked to take the Ernest Hemingway challenge and write a six-word story about ourselves. Legend has it the famed novelist introduced a short, short story — long before Twitter — by using six words: "For sale, Baby shoes, Never worn." After reflecting on my life from the time I was a child through a nearly 30-year career, I came up with my own six-word story: *"I'm Paula; I'll be your server."* That, too, is part of my brand.

Headlining Lisa's personal brand are integrity and fairness. She works hard and expects a lot from others — but nothing more than she expects of herself. At her core, she is a connector.

Lisa also started working at a young age and literally worked from the ground up. At 12 years old she was picking cucumbers and weeding peanut fields in rural Martin County, North Carolina. At 14, she was left to manage a garden nursery business and its employees, and she got her school bus driver's license when she got her regular driver's license — on her 16th birthday. When she went to pharmacy school at the University of North Carolina at Chapel Hill, and held down a 32-hour-a-week job at Eckerd Drugs while taking a full course load, those who knew her best were not at all surprised. Maybe it is her nature, or maybe it was born out of necessity, but Lisa is efficient, insightful and willing to take risks. She leads by example. She didn't realize it at the time, but she started building her brand as a leader while still a child and continued to hone it all the way to the C-suite.

Be Self-Aware

Sometimes in searching for your unique personal brand you will also stumble upon character traits that you don't want to be part of your brand. This information is also valuable. It leads to self-awareness, which is critical for growth.

Lisa discovered that being intense is part of who she is, but she didn't want that to overwhelm her brand. Sure, being intense can be great when you have tasks to accomplish, but it does not always bode well for personal relationships. Intensity can be intimidating. Recently, an acquaintance of 18 years confided to Lisa that she had never pursued a closer friendship because Lisa intimidated her. Lisa had no idea. She didn't intend to intimidate, but her success, confidence and *intensity* had, in fact, done just that. Lisa has a loud, authoritative voice, and it carries. She has learned she can communicate her brand more effectively if she talks a little softer and asks more questions instead of charging in with answers. But this requires effort.

As for me, through feedback from peers, I learned I was viewed as defensive. Gene Klann, my instructor at the Center for Creative Leadership, suggested I write a large "D" on my paper and color it, make it bold, whatever was necessary to keep that in my mind. It worked.

Even the most accomplished leaders need to keep growing. Lisa and I have more than 60 years of corporate experience, six decades of marriage, and nearly a half-century of parenting between us. We are still growing. But once you figure out what's helpful and what's harmful and put each in its proper place, you can use that self-awareness to harness your strengths. And that can help you break bad habits that may be holding you back. It can also give you a greater depth of knowledge and wisdom and is more likely to lead to that next promotion … and better relationships in your personal life, too.

You will be amazed at the balance, sense of fulfillment and career success that come with being true to your personal brand. Conversely, if you are not self-aware you will keep making the same mistakes over and over, and *your* brand will erode or become something you do not want it to be. Protect your brand.

Package Your Potential

Once you know your brand, you can focus on packaging your potential. It helps to have a career plan and know where you want to go and what you want to become. But if you haven't gotten that far, work on finding your sweet spot because that is where your potential lies.

When coaching others in making career decisions, we often use a Venn diagram to illustrate how to figure this out. Ask yourself three questions:

What am I passionate about?
What am I good at?
What can I make money doing?

Where these things intersect is your sweet spot — where you are most likely to be successful. Now you can focus your efforts on putting your best self forward and finding the right fit.

If your goal is to get that next promotion and become an executive, you need to start acting like it now. Having "stretch goals" will help you get there. Don't look just one step ahead; look two or three steps forward and be ready to stretch when the opportunity arises.

After I moved into the sales division of my company and realized how much I liked sales, I was ready to grow. When my boss's boss left the company, I was encouraged to go for the top role: vice president of sales. I knew leapfrogging my current boss was a big jump and potentially awkward, but I had worked hard and was prepared to go for it. I was also prepared not to get it, but I wanted to try. Stretching myself and taking the risk paid off. I got the job.

Don't overlook the things that seem little but can produce big returns. We are big believers in Harvard Business School Social Psychologist Amy Cuddy's theory on body language and "faking it until you become it." In her wildly popular TED Talk she shares her research on how "high power poses," as opposed to "low power poses," can influence not only our own brains but how others perceive us. These poses affect our presence and can project confidence, passion and authenticity. She also takes the common "fake it until you make it" mantra one step further and encourages people not to settle for just "making it" but to "fake it until you become it" — and you can. Unlock your high power pose and help others see your potential.

Build Your Network (Hint: It's Not All About You)

The impact of a strong network cannot be overstated. A good network, and we are talking quality over quantity, has the power to boost not just your career but your whole life. Just look at Lisa and me — we are living proof of the power of a network.

After years of competing fiercely for the same multimillion-dollar pharmaceutical contracts, and therefore not liking each other very much, our paths diverged and we were no longer going head-to-head. A mutual colleague attending a trade conference was the connector we needed.

"You need to meet Lisa Grimes," someone said. *"You two would really get along and enjoy each other."*

I may have had my doubts about that, but putting our previous perceptions and bouts of intimidating each other aside, we agreed to a lunch in 2002. We talked; we laughed; we finished each other's sentences. In each other, we found a kindred spirit, a sounding board, another woman who understood the trials of being an executive, a wife and a mother. Now we have written a book and hit the speaking circuit together. We definitely hit the networking jackpot!

Before Lisa, I had always networked within the company, but I now see the value in building one outside. As the only woman on my company's executive team, I never had a real sounding board, certainly no other woman who could understand where I was coming from. But building a network outside the company allowed me to talk about issues without worrying that the answer might be politically motivated or that confidential information was being shared.

Lisa and I not only understand where the other is coming from, we appreciate and understand what drives each other morally, ethically and intellectually. We hear each other without judging; we are comfortable asking tough questions that might cause us to think a little differently; we can shoot off a text and say, *"Do you think that's smart? Do you think there's a better way? Do you know anybody?"* And most important, we have a deep respect for each other.

Here is the most important thing we have learned about networking: *In a good network relationship, you are looking out for the other person's best interests. It's not all about you.*

Let's repeat that: It's not all about you. It's about the give and take. The best networking people we know are people who help other people in their network. They are connectors. The beauty of effective networking is that you are happy to introduce people you feel good about, people you think have integrity, people who will represent you well when you make that introduction. A solid network is the most effective way of finding a job, getting a promotion, landing a board seat or whatever the next thing is on your agenda.

Having said that, here are some of our favorite do's and don'ts when networking.

DO:
- Be yourself.
- Be honest.
- Be sincere.
- Be reciprocal (don't always take).
- Build a network that includes people with whom you have things in common and people who are different from you and will challenge your thinking.
- Use your network to grow your network.

DON'T:
- Overuse your network.
- Call on your network only when you want something.
- Use someone's name as a reference or a way to connect unless that person gives you permission.
- Talk more than you listen.

True story #1: My husband's ex-colleague knew of me, but I barely knew her and knew nothing of her work ethic. She came to my company to look for a job and used my name, unbeknownst to me. Then when I wouldn't help her get a job she started harassing me via email. Yes, these crazy things happen, and they're the best way to torpedo any chance of building an effective network. I do not often recommend someone for a job, but I frequently encourage someone to ask for a meeting and tell them they can use my name. But I better have given permission to use my name.

Conversely, if I do allow someone to use my name, a little consideration goes a long way.

True story #2: I once heard from an old college friend via LinkedIn, after 20 years of no contact. I was excited she had reached out to me after so long. She asked about my career, my family — she seemed genuinely interested in re-connecting. It turns out her husband needed a job. Based on our past relationship, I helped him get an interview and we offered him a job. Great, right? Well, he turned down the job and I never heard anything from either one of them again. Aside from proving themselves to be anything but "friends," this was a definite network party foul. Don't ask for a favor if you aren't sure you want it. Regardless, be respectful and grateful, always. And one more thing. Don't be a fake. It's transparent in all the wrong ways.

Just as there are different levels in your company, there are different levels in your network. Think of it as a pyramid with different layers. You should establish a network within your group, a network outside your group but still within your company, a network in your larger industry and a network that is completely out of your area of expertise. Right now see if you can come up with a name(s) in each of those categories. If not, you know where to start building your network.

If you are struggling to make those connections, consider volunteering for a project or initiative, at work or in the community, that will expose you to new people. If you are searching for a way to connect with someone higher in your company, look for opportunities to take "appropriate" advantage of situations with senior level executives.

For example, if there is a charitable cause that you have a passion for, and you know an executive shares that passion, perhaps start to network through that route. But don't just pretend to suddenly have a profound interest in a particular cause.

Also, there's nothing wrong with trying to casually bump into an exec in the buffet line. But don't stalk these folks. If you think you're going too far to try to meet somebody, chances are, you are. And never, NEVER try to meet somebody just to get them to introduce you to somebody they know. Don't use people in your network that way. If you do, your network will shrivel. None of us enjoy being used, and most of us work hard to not let it happen a second time. Do your homework and find a connection; just make sure to be sincere.

Remember, your network can also help or hinder your personal brand. It does more good to have a network that is narrow and deep than wide and shallow. You can build that starting today by reaching out to someone and inviting them in.

Control Your Digital Footprint

We are all digital citizens. It is a fact of life. Our digital footprint, from web surfing to social media commenting to app usage, is tracked, shared and commercialized. But that doesn't mean we have no control over it. We can and should care about protecting our online reputation and put some effort into making sure it is positive. How much effort depends on your goals and, quite honestly, your brand.

Truth be told, Lisa and I have not actively promoted our personal brands online. Until recently, no Instagram, no Twitter, no Facebook. It's a personal preference. We have, however, maintained up-to-date and professional LinkedIn profiles, as this is part of the all-important network. Often women will ask us how to decide whom to accept and whom to reject on LinkedIn. It's hard to set hard and fast rules for everyone, but I will tell you I have rejected about a thousand invitations. For instance, I won't welcome a competitor if I think they just want to access my network. I generally don't accept recruiters because I don't want tongues wagging, "Is she looking?" at my company.

If you truly mean for LinkedIn to be an effective networking tool, you should maintain some discretion over your contacts. We do that to create value and promote ourselves by doing our jobs well. It has worked out for us.

At a minimum, you do need to be aware of your online reputation. We all know employers routinely search the internet to glean information they hope will tell them whether you will fit into their culture. Don't give them a reason to pass you over for a job, promotion or sale because of something they found online. Colleges offer entire courses on how to protect and build positive online reputations, most notably by creating and sharing great content. Publishing research, commenting on forums or penning pertinent blogs can be a great way to share your expertise and promote your personal brand. Our rule of thumb: Would this be something you would be proud to show your mother? Enough said.

Care About Your Appearance

Like it or not, appearance matters, and it is part of your brand. You may think it cliché, but the old adage is true: You get only one chance to make a first impression, whether it's on a job interview or with a client. It can show that you pay attention to detail … or don't.

Lisa learned that lesson early in her career when she was asked to go to a big sales convention with her boss. She excitedly went out and bought a new suit — fuchsia linen, very stylish at the time. She even bought matching lipstick. She was ready! Later, her boss's boss gently mentioned that clients pay attention to the whole package, his gaze lingering on her shoes, which were scuffed and worn. In this day and age you might think that is a bit nitpicky. But it was a detail that stood out in an unflattering way, and she was grateful for the constructive feedback. And she's been into really cool shoes since then!

No, we are not telling you to spend thousands of dollars on designer suits and shoes and become a Botox babe who keeps your specialist on speed dial. We are talking about putting your best self forward. Take care of the basics. Wear clothes that fit and have a few fashion-forward outfits, even if it's just a new scarf in the season's latest color. Comb your hair and don't have it wadded up as if you just got out of bed— yes, we've seen this. Keep your nails neat and clean. Even if you are not into makeup, a little lip gloss and mascara never hurt. Dress for the occasion. And the occasion is going to work. Executives notice. Ask yourself how you want to be noticed. "Professional" should be at the top of the list. If you are wondering whether the blouse is too low and the skirt and heels are too high, the answer is probably … yes.

Studies have long shown that the way you present yourself can play into whether you get that next promotion and even how much money you make. Recent research by sociologists Jaclyn Wong from the University of Chicago and Andrew Penner from the University of California at Irvine found that people who are rated attractive by an interviewer make, on average, 20 percent more than those found to be of average attractiveness. This is on par with what other studies have found.

But Wong and Penner took it a step further to try to determine what makes a person attractive. Is it an innate beauty or something we can influence? The study found that, for women, most of the attractiveness advantage came in simply being well-groomed. Things like applying makeup, styling hair and wearing clothes that fit and look nice on you accounted for nearly all of the salary differences for women of varying physical attractiveness. In other words, it's not the size of your nose or waistline that matters. There are tangible benefits to being well-groomed, male or female.

Caution: This is also an area for you to *Remember Who You Are*. You may dress professionally and appropriately and still find yourself being encouraged to be someone you are not, whether by peers, customers or higher-ups. Not too long ago, a boss encouraged me to go buy a "disarmingly attractive" outfit for an important meeting. To this day, I am not quite sure what he had in mind, but after asking for advice from several peers and my business coach I did buy a nice designer suit — but I would call it tasteful, not disarming. I stayed true to myself … and the meeting went well.

Use Your Brand to Stay Balanced

If you have never considered your personal brand … do it now. We wish we had done it earlier in our careers. It is exciting to discover yourself. When your brand and your career goals are aligned, they can take you in a new direction or to new heights. If they are not aligned, you need to know sooner rather than later.

If you have a hard time handling rejection, a high-profile sales job probably isn't for you. If creativity and digital marketing are what makes you tick, being in a highly analytical position isn't going to lead to a fulfilling career. If being a person of integrity is important to your brand and you make it the filter through which you make decisions, then the next time you are pressed against the wall in a difficult situation, that decision won't be so tough. You will know what you need to do, you will be consistent and people will recognize and value that. Fulfillment, a sense of accomplishment, balance and peace come in knowing you have stayed true to yourself.

Dear Younger Laurie,

I know you're at a crossroads. You've just graduated from pharmacy school and have a plan for your life. However, you've met an MBA exchange student from a UK university during your last semester, and you've fallen head over heels in love. Your family and friends are skeptical, and even you are doubting the logic to marrying someone so very different from what you've known. In essence, you're wrestling with whether you should follow your heart or follow your head.

I can tell you that if you choose to follow your heart, things will work out beautifully! You will travel the world, have two incredible children who grow up to be confident global citizens, you will have a meaningful career, and perhaps most importantly, you will remain happily married to a man who is a true partner.

You will learn much with this life choice, and I hope this letter provides you with reassurance to trust your gut. You will continue to face numerous opportunities, and I'd like to share a few suggestions that I believe you can leverage in making decisions that will achieve a meaningful life.

✓ **Learn to like organizational politics.** You'll better understand why things happen and improve your ability to influence your career trajectory if you take an interest in who's who and read the company tea leaves. Plus you'll be an asset to others with your ability to provide context to what's going on.

✓ **Don't be afraid to not have all the answers.** If you're reluctant to speak up for fear that others must already know the answer, you're not giving those around you the benefit of what you do know and how you think. Your question might be the spark to help someone realize there are logic gaps, or even stimulate another idea.

✓ **A chameleon is a viable leadership style.** By moving on a career lattice instead of a ladder, you will learn how the industry is connected and gain important diverse perspectives. The future will need people who are agile learners to quickly adapt to current needs. Your curiosity and willingness to change are authentic.

✓ **Not everyone has to like you.** You will actually be of greater service to those around you if you're more willing to speak your mind, take a path less traveled, and provide critical feedback with a compassionate twist. I know you've been raised to be a good girl, but well-behaved women rarely make history.

✓ **Surround yourself with people who are better than you.** They will push you to maintain an "A" game, and enable you to be part of extraordinary teams. Your strength is in creating commitment, and you can't do it all yourself, so dream big and have confidence that your team's success is your success.

✓ **Girlfriends are essential.** While your husband is your best friend, there are innumerable benefits to spending time with amazing women. This network will open your eyes to the need to "build your well before you're thirsty." You will be a supporter to so many by drawing a wider circle in your life.

✓ **You don't need to plan your career.** Too many things can change. The best way I found for advancement is to look for the "sweet spot". This is the intersection where your passion, your talent, and the company's needs meet. Make your interests known. People can't help you if they don't know what you want.

And when you look around at other people and see all the different ways they're leading and succeeding, remember what Oscar Wilde said: "Be yourself; everyone else is already taken."

With much love and respect,
The Later Laurie

Laurie Cooke
CEO
Healthcare Businesswomen's Association

2

Delivering X Plus

"Overcome the notion that you must be regular. It robs you of the chance to be extraordinary."

~ Uta Hagen

by Lisa

For a girl who couldn't sew and couldn't cook and whose worst grade in school was in home economics, it is a little odd that I had a green thumb. But I did. At 13 years old, I was working in a garden nursery in rural Martin County, rooting plants and helping customers. If I was asked to water, I would weed too. Yes, there was the time I overfertilized 500 azalea plants and they burned up, but the owners were willing to overlook my zeal in feeding the Southern staple of springtime. In fact, when they went on vacation they put me in charge of the nursery and its employees for a week. I was 14 then. That was probably a little crazy, but they viewed me as reliable and trustworthy, and I was oh-so-eager to prove myself and impress them. Never mind that I drove the onsite truck through the greenhouse while they were gone (I was only 14!). That was such a great job. I learned many life lessons caring for plants and customers at the nursery — like what can happen when you go above and beyond what is expected of you, and how perseverance pays off.

By the time I graduated from pharmacy school at the University of North Carolina at Chapel Hill, I had decided I was more interested in selling pharmaceuticals than dispensing them. I didn't think this would be a problem. After all, I had done an internship with a large pharmaceutical company.

I began sending out applications for sales jobs. One by one, the rejections came back. *No thank you. You need a different degree. You need different experiences.* Sometimes I got an interview, but never the job. It was always the same response: *You don't have any sales experience. You can work in QC.*

After I had been turned down 23 times — yes, 23 times — I decided I needed to take a different tack. When I went to interview at Beecham and received the common refrain about my lack of experience, I asked as politely as I could, "Were you born with sales experience? How do I get it if nobody will give me a chance?" And then I said: "I have an offer for you. I will sign any legal contract you want that says I will pay you back every bit of money you pay me if I don't overperform in six months. No one has sales experience until they are given the chance."

Well, they gave me the chance (and didn't make me sign the contract), but it took being pretty bold to even get my foot in the door.

Now it was time to deliver what I promised "plus," which I did by exceeding my sales goal.

Paula and I both come from families that instilled the idea of *Delivering X Plus*, or, as Paula's dad liked to say, "Give 110 percent!" It's a practice her PawPaw "Bax" lived by as well, and not surprisingly, it built his reputation around town as a restaurateur and became part of his personal brand. It has worked for us, and it can help you achieve success too.

As executives, we see clearly that there are two groups of people: those who deliver X, whom we'll call individual contributors, and those who deliver X plus, our solution providers. Most people are not X plus. One of the most important pieces of advice we give to people starting out or looking to advance is, if you want an upwardly mobile career instead of just a job, be in the X plus crowd.

Establish Credibility

When I told that interviewer I would overperform in six months for the "I've never done sales before" job, I had no idea what I was getting into. It turns out I was put into a territory with negative sales. Negative sales? I didn't even know that was possible. But yes, when product is returned and credited back — it is possible — you need to sell more than your goal just to break even! I had my work cut out for me, but I also had an opportunity to establish myself. There were plenty of lessons learned:

Make an action plan. For me, that meant putting in extra hours learning about the products and customers and learning how to sell so when I met clients I could more easily figure out what they wanted. I did that over and over again with client after client. No one told me to put in 110 percent — I had to motivate myself to do it. Paula encourages employees looking to advance to "time box" a plan for success. For instance, spend 6-12 months deeply understanding your role and your manager's expectations, and set your personal goals. Spend at least the next 12 months executing, delivering and exceeding those goals. In the following 6-12 months, continue to do your job well and start seeking your next challenging role, before boredom or complacency sets in.

Be a solution provider. A question gets an answer; a problem gets a solution. Be the employee who offers a solution instead of simply answering a question.

I always think of Al as a great example of a solution provider. I hired Al as a sales guy because he was highly intelligent and wasn't afraid to challenge the status quo; he was not a yes-man. Still, I was skeptical when he came to me and said he thought our normal way of making a pitch to a sponsor company would not be enough to win a particular contract. It was a highly competitive business, and he was convinced we needed to do something innovative to close the deal. However, he didn't just come into my office and state the problem. He went the extra mile of coming up with a solution — and had already met with a potential partner that agreed to change its normal way of doing business to deliver what we needed for our pitch. So we revamped our entire sales pitch and made a proposal that was completely different from anything anyone else was offering — or anything we had offered in the past. We won the contract, and I'm convinced it was because I had a solution provider like Al on my team. I wish there were more Al's in the world.

It is worth noting that the one who stands out is not necessarily the one who works more hours; it's the one who achieves more. *Hint:* The phrase "it's not my job" should never cross your lips if you are looking to advance your career.

Differentiate yourself. Find a way to set yourself apart from your competitors. You do that when you:

- Leverage unlikely skill sets. (I am a pharmacist, an interior designer, and a CEO; Paula is a statistician who became a business developer on her way to the executive suite.)

- Offer an added benefit your boss or client isn't expecting. (When you put a little extra nugget in that proposal.)
- Become known for something memorable. (Paula's penchant for Krispy Kreme donuts has earned her a box left on conference tables from Kansas City to Tokyo; my taste for hot sauce has earned me deliveries of bottles so hot I have had to sign a waiver before breaking the seal.)

One of the best ways to differentiate yourself is through show and tell. It is not enough to just *tell* your boss or client what you will do (which is what most people do); you need to *show* them how you can apply your life/work experiences to their needs or to do the job. For instance, I would not just tell a client that we have done 10 similar research projects. I would show them that *because* we have done that, we have learned *XYZ* and will use that information to generate the best results for them. When Paula was leading a team to bring a new diabetes drug to market, she participated in an FDA Advisory Committee meeting. Being involved in the approval pipeline end-to-end allowed her to *show* her knowledge of the process and *tell* stories of how best to submit, respond, and approach that process.

Setting yourself apart from your competitors will cement your credibility with others and put you ahead of the pack.

Grow Your Root Ball

Gazing out her office window one dreary, rainy day, Paula waited for a member of her team to arrive for a meeting. Mike was looking for advice on how to develop his career. She had been encouraging him to take on a new role in a different area, but he was reluctant. As she watched the stands of tall pines swaying in the wind, she half expected them to snap. But instead there was a "pop" — in her head, like a light bulb. She knew how she would explain to Mike the value of building his skill set and expanding his area of expertise. Her root ball analogy was born.

If you broaden your knowledge and experience, you will grow your root ball — your base will widen, and you will be able to withstand any storm (merger, reorganization, new business initiative). If you specialize in just one area, you may have a narrow root ball and you may grow tall and thin like a pine tree, ready to snap in bad weather. Eventually you may find it difficult even to make a lateral move. Yes, there are exceptions for specific skill sets.

Make time to grow your root ball. Take advantage of every learning opportunity, whether it is attending a conference, taking an online course or webinar, or even volunteering for a new initiative or responsibility in your office.

Before Paula even graduated from college she started as employee No. 23 at a start-up. She was an entry-level statistician. When she left that company some 30 years later, it had grown to 35,000 employees and she was second to the CEO of a Fortune 500 business. In the interim she had worn more hats than most people who jump from company to company. She didn't do that simply by working hard and turning her reports in on time. She was always growing her root ball.

Seize the moment. It was the summer of 1987, a steamy day in Chicago, when Paula found herself in a stretch limousine on the way to a client's office with her entrepreneurial CEO.

"How are you getting along?" he asked. "Are you enjoying your job?"

Although she was just 23 years old, Paula seized the opportunity to tell her boss that what she really wanted was the opportunity to travel and to be considered for roles elsewhere, if the company ever opened an office outside of North Carolina. One year later, she found herself in a new London-based office for a yearlong assignment. Although she went over to serve as a "stats girl," the office of eight people soon provided greater opportunities. She jumped in to help as a project manager, an office manager, a business developer. She hired people, dealt with vendors and went on sales calls. In short, she established herself as being the go-to girl and demonstrated management ability. Her root ball was spreading outward and downward, and she was able to carry that back to the States. Some 28 years later, before she left the company as president of the clinical division, she had also served as an executive in project management, business development/sales, and operations. Of course, today she uses those experiences as a business coach, consultant, board member, author, and speaker, so the roots are still running and spreading.

Missed expectations. There might come a time when you overpromise and underdeliver or miss someone's expectations. The key is not to let that happen more than once. Paula learned this lesson early in life. She recalls:

This crotchety old teacher, in his tweed jacket and glasses, would lumber into the family restaurant every morning precisely at 10:30 a.m. for his coffee break. Every day it was the same thing — coffee, black, 35 cents a cup, unlimited refills — and he had many. One day I overfilled his cup and a bit of coffee spilled in his saucer. Later, when clearing the table, I found that he had left a penny tip. The ultimate insult. Of course, I was furious about his pettiness, but I got the message … I missed his expectation, and the penny tip was the consequence. I learned a valuable lesson from old Professor J that I carried into my career.

How well you do a task matters — even a small task. Do you do a high quality job? More or less than is expected?

Reveal Grit

As the new head of business development, I was sent with my one and only sales person, whom I had hired the week before, to make a pitch to an international company at its U.S. headquarters. When we walked into the large board room, 12 men were lined up on one side of the table, with the two of us on the other side. It was a firing squad … literally. We were there to pitch a multimillion-dollar sales contract, and they were there to discuss the less than stellar job the company had done on prior work. We had no idea there even was prior work. Suffice it to say, I wanted to sink into the floor as I listened to their litany of complaints and issues. I had two choices: I could mumble quick apologies and scoot out with my tail between my legs, or dig deep and try to salvage the relationship. I chose the latter. I chose grit.

Grit is often referred to as the intersection of passion and perseverance. Tenacity, fortitude, determination; call it what you will, but it's part of an unwillingness to give up — the drive to work hard to achieve a goal. Psychologist Angela Lee Duckworth, author of the best-selling book *Grit: The Power of Passion and Perseverance*, has brought the term into a new vogue by touting the effective use of her grit scale — a set of survey questions that tests one's willingness to persevere in pursuit of long-term goals. She concludes that grit is one of the leading predictors of success — even over talent. She also believes we all have the ability to increase our level of grit.

While studies and research on these sweeping claims continue to evolve, we can tell you, as business executives — not psychologists — that grit as a character trait has indeed fostered success for us, and we believe it can do the same for you.

I did, in fact, manage not only to salvage the relationship with our international client but to make the sale I came to make. Grit.

X Plus Delivers

After years of unsuccessful fertility treatments and being told I would never have children, I decided to throw myself into work and landed my dream job. Great! Within a month, I found out I was pregnant. Even greater! Although it wasn't ideal timing in terms of my career, my husband and I were beyond thrilled at our unexpected blessing, and I wasn't about to shortchange myself. I wanted 6 months off — double the standard maternity leave where I was working. But when I made the request, I also had a proposed solution. I offered to take phone calls for the last three months of requested leave and agreed to attend a few key events that allowed me to keep my baby with me. My new boss agreed. I believe he was willing to work with me because I had established credibility, delivered X plus and offered a solution and not just a problem.

The benefits of *Delivering X Plus* can pay dividends not just in job promotions, and marketability, but in quality of life as well. If you are willing to go above and beyond for others, others are more likely to go above and beyond for you. It's really pretty simple. It's not the letters behind your name (or lack thereof) that will be your biggest propellant; it's what you put into it and how you treat others. Networking is good for making a connection, getting an interview, and maybe even getting the job. But your network generally doesn't keep you in the job or get you promoted. Our 70-20-10 rule of thumb to achieve success:

- 70 percent overdelivering to get the job done,
- 20 percent using an effective network (internal and external),
- 10 percent continuing your education.

As executives, we can tell you we gravitate toward the employees who deliver X plus and seek them out for promotions and new opportunities. Take Paula's experience with Rich. As she describes it:

When I hired Rich to do the financial accounting for my team, I secretly wondered whether I could handle his brash Brooklyn accent. The term "Yankee" always came to mind when I saw him in the hallway. File that under "never judge a book by its cover." Rich turned out to be one of the best hires I ever made. He did more than just report on revenue and profits. He learned the operational side of the business too, not because he had to, but because he thought he would do a better job if he understood the details of the operation. I assumed he was looking to prepare himself for a CFO position, but two years later when I was looking for a head of operations, I immediately thought of him.

"Me?" he asked. "I'm a lifelong finance guy. Are you sure you want to do this?"

"Absolutely!" I replied. "I think it will help you grow, and you will learn it."

I thoroughly trusted him. He took it upon himself to learn new things and gave so much more than anyone asked him to. Rich is now the senior vice president of a large company overseeing operations. He took me to lunch recently and thanked me for giving him the opportunity to "grow his root ball." He also shared that when he was in high school he won the "110% Award" on his varsity basketball team — first one to the gym, last one to leave. Go figure.

The moral of the story? Give 110 percent and watch your career (and life) blossom.

Dearest Shideh,

Guess what? You are going to do okay—in fact, more than okay! And all the self-doubt, the anxiety, the knots in your stomach, the lost sleep—they don't add much value, so you might as well add a few years to your life by giving up that self-torture and pay more attention to enjoying the ride. Oh yes, it will have BIG highs and big lows, but that is why people stand in line for roller coasters, isn't it? Be one of those people who sit in the front car and throw their hands up in the air!

Give as many new things a try as you can, and try not to shut things down from further exploration. You know, like never taking an art class again after 8th grade because you decided you "just don't have any artistic ability". Keep those doors open for more exploration – or one day you'll look up and 45 years have passed and you haven't picked up a crayon or a marker and drawn for the heck of it, just to see where the crayon takes you. What a loss.

And remember that advice your Mom gave you. When she said "I know you are going to be successful; just keep in mind your success is only worthwhile if it elevates the life of another. So, if your cousin really needs or even wants something they can't afford and you can – buy it for them." Following that advice will give you some of the deepest and most satisfying moments in your life!

Set sail, leave the harbor of certainty, have fun and – yes – exercising along the way and eating well is important, except when you are in Italy or France, in which case GO FOR IT!

With all my love and respect,
Me

Shideh Sedgh Bina
Founding Partner
Insigniam

3

Authentic Leadership

"The challenge of leadership is to be strong, but not rude; be kind, but not weak; be bold, but not bully; be thoughtful, but not lazy; be humble, but not timid; be proud, but not arrogant; have humor, but without folly."

~ Jim Rohn

by Paula

"One, two, three o'clock, four o'clock rock. Five, six, seven o'clock, eight o'clock rock." Toe tapping, be-bopping and big smiles filled the room as the tunes of Bill Haley & His Comets wailed through the cafeteria. *"Nine, ten, eleven o'clock, twelve o'clock rock. We're going to rock around the clock*

tonight." It was Employee Appreciation Day, a tradition started to build pride and camaraderie in our ranks — a way to say thank you. More than a thousand people came for lunch and games, team building and awards. Some executives participated; some did not. We weren't forced to. And, when I was asked to emcee the 50's-themed event, I said yes without hesitation. I rented a poodle skirt and even learned how to skateboard so I could make my grand entrance on wheels. I was greeted with laughter, applause, and appreciation from the crowd. I showed up.

Connecting outside the confines of the cubicle and the conference room was my way of showing I cared about our employees beyond what they could do to make the company successful. It's why I went to weddings and funerals. It's why I stayed at holiday parties from beginning to end. It's why I had company bibs made and delivered with a handwritten note when one of my employees had a baby. Webster's defines authentic as being genuine or real; being true to oneself. There are many types of leaders and many different leadership styles. For me, striving to be an authentic leader is the only thing that makes sense. It is part of my personal brand. It is at the core of remembering who I am. It is a philosophy Lisa and I share.

Make A Connection

If you travel enough, you end up with a good airplane story. Maybe you reconnect with someone from your past or make a new connection that affects your future. If you close your laptop, take off your headphones and make yourself available to "connect," you never know what might happen. A career-changing connection and a lifelong mentor emerged for Lisa on a Boeing 747. Her story:

> *I was en route from Raleigh to New York City to speak at a conference when I started chatting with a friendly, older gentleman across the aisle. As it turns out, he was going to the same conference. He began asking questions, questions about me, insightful questions about our*

industry; I did a lot of talking to this man I had just met. "He's a really great listener," I thought.

As the conversation went on, I was impressed how "real" this guy seemed. He was not at all egotistical although clearly intelligent, and he did not talk about himself or drop any names. As it turns out, he was the vice president of a major pharmaceutical company. At the time, I was an assistant dean at the UNC School of Pharmacy, having jumped off the corporate track in hopes of getting pregnant — although by this point, fertility doctors were giving us no hope of conceiving.

The gentleman from the plane ended up coming to hear me speak at the conference and afterward gave me his card and told me to call for an appointment if I had any interest in rejoining the corporate world. The timing was right, and the opportunity to work for this man, or rather, work several layers below him, turned out to be one of the best moves of my career. He showed me what an authentic leader looked like, acted like and sounded like. It can't be faked. It must be real. He was what Jim Collins describes in his best-selling book From Good To Great as a Level 5 leader. I knew immediately that is also what I wanted to be.

Humility

Collins describes a Level 5 leader as someone who combines humility with fierce resolve — a potent mix that separates "good" from "great." And people want to work with Level 5 leaders because they put people over power. When leaders show humility and their own humanity, they are connecting with employees in a way other leaders cannot.

In a study by the University of Washington Foster School of Business, in which employees rated supervisors on humility and their own job satisfaction, Associate Professor Michael Johnson found that those who rated their managers as more humble reported feeling more engaged and less likely to leave the organization.

We have been leaders and we have been led, and we can testify this is true. When leaders seek success that elevates the team and the company over themselves, when they share credit and accept blame, Level 5 leadership and corporate success will follow.

This is not easy. In fact, oftentimes being humble goes against a person's very nature, especially in our social-media-saturated culture, which encourages a sort of narcissism in every tweet, post and selfie. For women who feel they are trying to make it in a "man's world," it can be even tougher. If we don't toot our own horns and take credit … who will do it for us? How will we get recognized? There is no doubt it takes *courage* to practice humility, but Johnson's and Collins' findings are clear: Humility is a competitive advantage and a leading indicator of success. Even if you are not a naturally humble person you can learn to be, Johnson says, just as a person can learn to become more patient.

"If we focus on appreciating the strengths of others, focus on being teachable, having an accurate view of ourselves, we can actually become more humble people," Johnson writes.

Build a team. Successful leaders surround themselves with successful people. We don't know everything — not even close. But if we can bring together a group with complementary skill sets (sales, tech, etc.) and we let people work in their sweet spots, a great synergy emerges. This set-up naturally allows us to show humility by giving us the opportunity to acknowledge team members' strengths and lift them up knowing their success will be ours, and vice versa. When we hire those competent and experienced people we also need to be willing to listen to their ideas and advice — another opportunity to connect and show humility. It's exactly what Lisa's mentor displayed on that brief encounter on the plane … the virtue of listening. Two of Lisa's top employees right now have worked with her at four companies. She has shown them humility and authentic leadership, and they have rewarded her with loyalty. She builds great teams with these people. Not coincidentally, these are people who often have distinguished themselves as being in the X plus crowd. Have we mentioned how valuable they are?

*Tip: It can be a challenge to assemble that great team. We suggest following your gut instinct. Women actually excel at this, and it can give them an advantage in being effective leaders. Look for a connection with a potential hire beyond the resume. If your gut is saying, *Thanks, but no thanks*, listen to it. If you have a mishire — and it happens — document it, draw your line in the sand, and move decisively so you don't risk bringing down the whole team and the chemistry you have worked to build.

> *"As a leader, when you make a mistake, own it. It will restore people's confidence and increase your influence."*
> — Michael Hyatt

Take responsibility. Of course, it is easy to appear a great leader in the good times, especially if you are *humble* enough to stand in the shadows and shine the light on your team. But as is often the case in life, it is how you handle the bad times that will define you as a leader. It is another opportunity to stand out as a truly authentic leader. Another Lisa story:

There's no worse feeling than standing before your board of directors with disappointing sales numbers. I know because I've been there. No matter how aggressive the goals, no matter how hard your team works, no matter what extenuating circumstances may exist, at the end of the day the numbers are black and white and someone needs to take responsibility. As the head of the team or company, that someone is me.

When my international sales team failed to meet a critical goal for the young company that employed us, I could have pointed a finger at others — but that was not the kind of leader I wanted to be. I believed in my team, and we were in it together. I went to the board and provided a systematic analysis of why "we" missed our goal AND provided ideas of how "we" could fix it.

What response did I get from the board?

"We appreciate you being transparent and appreciate you coming up with solutions to overcome the challenges," they said.

My team also appreciated that I did not throw them under the bus and that I had their backs. It motivated all of us to roll up our sleeves and work harder to make sure it didn't happen again.

It may seem counterintuitive, but when you are willing to shoulder the responsibility, you actually increase your influence and restore everyone's confidence — bosses, customers and employees. They will continue to look to you for guidance. That display of integrity, sincerity, and transparency results in loyal employees who are willing to double down to succeed. That's authentic leadership.

Our friend Debra Morgan, Emmy Award winning anchor, WRAL-TV, says it this way:

∾

Integrity and trust are qualities integral to my career and my life. I often tell young journalism students we are human, we make mistakes. It's how you handle the mistake that matters. Be open and honest with your peers, your audience and most importantly, yourself.

Routinely during a newscast while playing a taped story, the anchors are communicating with the producer about the show through an earpiece and our microphone. One night, we continued beyond the end of the taped piece and I responded to her question completely unrelated to the story being aired. Unfortunately, people at home heard me say, ON-AIR, "Oh, who cares" as the taped piece ended with the subject of the story succumbing to her long struggle with cancer. The phones, understandably, started ringing off the hook. After the next commercial break, I apologized. Regardless of the innocence of the error, I messed up and I owned it. The viewers responded with overwhelming kindness. Trust. It's hard to obtain and it goes away quickly if you don't respect it.

So why is it so hard for women, especially, to say "I'm sorry, my bad"? I've worked with a few over the years who rarely, if ever, accepted responsibility for failures. It diminishes their credibility. I'd much rather work with someone who's willing to say — "I made a mistake, I blew it." That's someone you can rely on to offer their honest opinion about themselves and others; good, bad and ugly. Accept responsibility and grow from a mistake, don't hide from it.

అ

Confidence

Whenever I speak to a group of women, there is one question that is always asked, always.

"What would you do differently?"

My answer is always the same, always.

"I wish I had been more confident earlier in my career."

Looking back, I can say I was defensive in meetings because I wasn't confident enough. I fell into the trap of competing with other women because I wasn't confident enough. Because there were no letters behind my name in an industry filled with PhDs and MDs, I was not confident enough. As it turns out, I was far from alone. In fact, I was a statistic.

Journalists Katty Kay and Claire Shipman explore what they call "The Confidence Gap" in their book, *The Confidence Code: The Science and Art of Self-Assurance — What Women Should Know*. When they interviewed dozens of influential women all over the world, they found that nearly all of them suffer from self-doubt. They share such startling findings as:

- A Carnegie Mellon study found that men initiate salary increase discussions four times more than women and for 30 percent more money than the women who do ask for a salary negotiation. Why? The women lack confidence.

- A study by social psychologist Brenda Major at the University of California-Santa Barbara found that men consistently overestimated their abilities and performance to do a task while women underestimated themselves, although their performances did not differ in quality. Why? Lack of confidence.

- Hewlett Packard discovered that women in their company apply for promotions only if they feel they are 100 percent qualified for a position, as opposed to men who apply even if they think they are only 60 percent qualified. Why? Lack of confidence.

If I am a statistic, Lisa is the exception. She will tell you, *"I don't think I was qualified for any job I ever got. I could never check every box — but it never stopped me from trying."* Of course, that is part of what makes her a great leader.

The conclusion: Many women feel confident only when they are perfect … or practically perfect.

The problem: None of us is Mary Poppins.

This can be a real career-breaker for women because research evidence shows that *confidence is just as important as competence in achieving success.* That is a critical point to understand and digest. University of California-

Berkeley psychologist Cameron Anderson has found that overconfident people — those who appeared the most self-assured even if they were NOT the most knowledgeable and capable — were routinely the most admired and highly regarded in an organization. Confidence, he says, is a part of your talent; you will need it to navigate the corporate jungle.

There are both nature and nurture explanations offered for women's tendency to be deficient in the confidence department. Testosterone has been linked to power and risk-taking behavior, while estrogen encourages bonding and connection — which are good things, but discourage risk-taking. On the nurture side of things, Stanford psychologist Carol Dweck has taken the TED Talk circuit by storm describing her work on a growth mindset (willingness to take risks and fail) vs. a fixed mindset (reluctance to try for fear of failure). She has found that when girls are praised for being "perfect" in grade school, they are inadvertently being conditioned into a fixed mindset where they become fearful of failure and avoid taking risks, so as not to jeopardize their "perfect" record. However, after decades of study, psychologists now believe risk-taking, failure and perseverance are essential to confidence building. And without confidence, you cannot be a great leader, authentic or otherwise.

The good news: Confidence can be built. "The Confidence Gap" can be closed. Ohio State University psychology professor Richard Petty told Kay and Shipman, "Confidence is the stuff that turns thoughts into actions."

I learned this firsthand when I shifted from project management to sales. Although I stayed with the same company for 30 years, I was always looking for new opportunities within the company, so when a sales path opened I jumped at the chance. I felt as if I had done sales in some fashion for most of my life, ever since I went door-to-door selling fruitcakes for the Civitan Club when I was 10 years old. But that career path didn't go as well as I had hoped, initially. Although I had sales skills, I lacked confidence. I began to think maybe it was a good time to take a sabbatical year.

Fortunately, I had a mentor who discouraged me from stepping back and instead encouraged me to "lean in" — to borrow an apt phrase from Facebook COO Sheryl Sandberg. So, I signed up for a weeklong sales course in Atlanta. After many lectures and workshops, the 12 attendees had to "sell" their product to a "buyer" (the course instructor). I won "The Order"! I left that sales course with more knowledge, a plaque (which I have kept to this day) and, most important, a big boost in confidence. So much so that not long after that I put my name forward for head of sales and leap-frogged a level to get the job. I never would have had the faith in myself to go for that job or even stay in sales if I hadn't taken action to build confidence.

In other words, stop thinking so much and just act! You can turn that vicious cycle of low confidence, resulting in inaction, into a virtuous cycle of building confidence by taking action, even if it means taking some risks or perhaps failing.

Take risks. When I promised a new customer that we would complete a New Drug Application (NDA) for a massive regulatory submission in less than half the time it usually takes, my team grew anxious and skeptical. "What is she thinking?" they asked one another. I knew it was a huge undertaking, but we had an opportunity to bring a new medicine to market and create a valuable partnership. I also knew it was an opportunity to give my team "stretch goals" and accomplish something big. "This is how careers are made," I told them.

We mapped out an aggressive timeline and got to work. I was with them every step of the way, including at the office — all night long — the night before our deadline, helping with whatever needed to be done. The application was hand delivered to the FDA in Maryland without a moment to spare. It was exhilarating.

There is no doubt that taking on that project was both risky and bold, but it paid off. It built confidence among every member of the team and gave them more confidence in me as a leader, not to mention that it cemented our relationship with a new client. I was on my way to becoming a more authentic leader because I signed up the team and showed up to ensure we delivered as a team. Talk about confidence building!

Analysis paralysis. This is a problem we see often, especially with women, and it erodes our confidence in ourselves and in how we are viewed by others. We want to be 100 percent prepared, 100 percent ready, 100 percent sure. But while we toil over being 100 percent sure, overanalyzing things and not taking action, our male counterparts have already made a decision and run with it.

We have used the 80/20 rule to help make decisions and avoid analysis paralysis. The Pareto Principle states that 80 percent of the results come from 20 percent of the causes. We apply that concept to being willing to make decisions when we have 80 percent or more of the information in hand. We might be wrong 20 percent of the time, but we might be right 80 percent of the time. The point is we made a decision.

The risk of not making a decision could be that it is made for you. Not only could it be a bad decision, but it could cost you control and respect as a leader. Have we mentioned that perfectionism is a confidence killer? Definitely be prepared, but let go of the need to be perfect. It will only hold you back and create inner turmoil.

To speak or not to speak? Business meetings can be filled with land mines for women. If you talk too much (or too loudly), people label you as aggressive or defensive. If you don't talk enough, people think you lack confidence or value. If you find yourself apologizing and speaking in questions instead of statements, you sound unsure and insecure. It seems to be a lose-lose proposition, right? We have sat through more hours of meetings than we can count and have probably made every mistake you can make.

But we also learned some valuable lessons. First, when you want to say something, say it with authority and conviction, and if you can't speak with authority on a topic — don't. Do not apologize before or after you speak (we hear this A LOT with women). Have evidence — facts or examples — to back up your comments. Women often speak from their gut, which can be valuable, but be sure you offer more than your opinion. Don't fall into the trap of speaking out in a meeting just because you think your voice should be heard.

Here's some food for thought. Can you sit through an entire meeting without saying a word? Are you confident enough to do that? For many women in leadership positions, or aspiring to leadership positions, the answer is no. We are both guilty of this, so we understand you. We understand you feel the need to prove yourself. We understand the strong desire to validate your presence in an important decision-making meeting. We understand that your idea or comment *just had to be heard.*

But consider this: Sometimes silence is truly golden — and displays a deeper level of confidence. Remember Lisa's mentor, the authentic Level 5 leader who was such a great listener? What would happen if you focused more on listening and less on speaking? What would happen if you asked a few thoughtful questions instead of charging in with all the answers? Yes, this can be trickier for women than for men, but if you find yourself not accomplishing what you want in meetings, why not try a different approach?

Build Relationships

If you put in the effort to develop relationships with your team — showing up, making connections — it will afford you privileges and opportunities to go places you would not have gone otherwise. There will be no need for candy-coated conversations because you will be able to have candid conversations when it is time to push or challenge your team. You will also enjoy greater influence because that, too, is built on relationships.

Delegate with accountability. When I got my first job in management, my dad gave me this advice: "Don't let them put the monkey on your back." Although this conjured an odd visual, what he meant was, don't let your employees' problems become your problems. Coach people to solve their own problems instead of stepping in to fix the problems for them.

For many, delegating is tough. The tendency to micromanage and do everything yourself can be strong, especially if a team member is struggling. The old adage, "If you want something done right, you've got to do it yourself," is often credited to Napoleon Bonaparte, but we saw what happened to him. A better mantra might be, "If you want something done right, delegate it." Of course, this works best when you have built a good team.

Even more difficult than delegating, though, can be following through with accountability. A business coach once showed me how providing structure and setting boundaries — set measurable goals, achieve the goals, follow up on progress — can introduce discipline into a relationship where everyone wins. The follow-up may be something as informal as a periodic meeting or check-in (get it on your calendar or it may never happen), but including accountability in the relationship will give your team confidence in you as a leader, and in their own abilities. If they learn there is no accountability, not only will they stop listening to you, but you will lose credibility and respect, too.

Make unpopular decisions. There isn't much more unpopular than having to lay people off. Between mergers and reorganizations, I have had to lay off thousands of people. Yes, thousands, including 20-year veterans, a former boss, and my own brother-in-law. I'm not going to lie — it's never easy. I knew these decisions were made for the longevity of the company and the betterment of a larger group. I knew it wasn't personal. But I also knew it was personal for the person losing their job.

Here's what I found: If I carried out my responsibilities with confidence and empathy, if I bothered to build relationships with employees, if I showed authentic leadership in those difficult moments, people did not hold me personally responsible. Those same attitudes allowed me to move a member off the team if I recognized he/she was not going to make it to the next level, although I was almost always willing to help them find another job if I could. Bottom line: If you are willing to look out for others' best interests — the individual's and the company's — those tough conversations will happen and your influence and leadership will remain intact.

Be bold, but not bully. This is one of our favorite lines from business philosopher Jim Rohn's seven challenges of leadership. It is a reminder of the fine line many executives find themselves walking, and a great distinguisher among leaders. Getting it right is the difference between being a successful leader and a poor leader. Setting goals and pushing your team to reach them, as I did with our new drug submission, was bold. However, had I pushed too hard, had I ridiculed one of my team members in front of others, attacked someone's character, compared them to others or threatened them to do a specific task … that would have been bullying. Bullying not only destroys your team members' motivation, but they will lose confidence in your ability to lead. It sounds so basic. Everyone should understand that leaders shouldn't bully, right? We have seen many leaders — often those who are more worried about themselves than others — fall because they were perceived by their subordinates as bullies. People don't enjoy following bullies. They will not follow them for long.

*Tip: If you have a problem or concern with someone, address it in a private meeting, not in a team meeting or in front of others.

The truth is, people don't care how much you know (or don't know) if they don't know how much you care. Care about your people whether it is giving credit for a job well done, going to bat for them when the chips are down, inquiring about their lives or families or just being willing to engage them with humor once in a while. Get "real" and enjoy the benefits of being an authentic leader!

My Darling Daughter,

What a wonderful thing a career is. It happens all at once and over time. Somewhere along the way of working hard, worrying constantly and taking on greater responsibility — just when you think you can't do any more than you are doing — your "job" has become a career. A career is defined by Webster's as: *an occupation undertaken for a significant period of a person's life and with opportunities for progress.*

Over the years, you have said to me, "Don't worry, it will all work out. I'll be married to my career and travel the world." I'm glad that your vision of a career is that glamorous. And by the way, it can be. I would love nothing more than a "glamorous career" for you. Glamour can mean lots of things to lots of people.

This will not be an easy journey, but it will be a rewarding one! So, let's talk about what I might tell you to be mindful of as you navigate your path.

First, I will personally canonize the person who institutes a "do not say the word 'strategy' in an interview" rule. I am convinced it is the most overused and misunderstood word in the business world. So, my darling daughter, begin with this premise. STRATEGY WITHOUT EXECUTION IS HALLUCINATION.

Instead of focusing on the fact that you believe you're a strategist (because strategists execute), begin each day as you start your "career" with these simple ideas:

- **I will work harder.**
- **I will think more creatively.**
- **I will act with intense passion toward my work, my peers and my boss.**

In your mind, be very clear that the best jobs are fun because you love what you do, not because you do "fun things."

Remember that when you got to your internship you said you were worried about whether Berkeley was a good enough school and whether you were prepared enough to make a significant contribution.

It isn't about pedigree – it's about passion. Find it. Recognize what you do well and leverage it to help you determine what you do – not what you should do. One of my observations is that passion wins more times than not. Be clear that it must be wrapped in analytical support with a strong business case to fuel its growth. Passion needs power partners. Think your finance partner. Think HR.

These power partners will support you in your endeavors. As much as passion will gather people to support your work, you will need these partners — always.

Recognize as my father told me: Everyone has a vote. Just one vote! The president will vote at a critical time, and the janitor will vote at a critical time. You will need both.

As a woman, don't let the joy of passion and the intensity of purpose make you lose sight of the need for a pragmatic approach to ensure that you can convert vision to reality.

As a woman, don't focus on the need to prove you're the most service-oriented or the sweetest <u>woman</u> in the room. Those are attributes women are supposed to have that don't get you points or value in the workplace.

Focus on being the most in-tune <u>person</u> to the nuances of a meeting, a relationship, a circumstance, and turn those observations into valuable insights — attributes women do have that lead to workplace value.

One of my mentors observed that in meetings, female executives often take notes and are asked to share them. Male executives listen as if the room is presenting to them alone, and they have no intention of being the "note taker or sharer." When you get to be an executive ... don't be the note taker.

Your value as a woman is that you will:

- Innately sense when things are right or wrong: Take a position.
- Be more approachable and therefore capable of building stronger relationships: Foster them — up and down.
- Create collaboration through your treatment of others rather than by a concerted effort of process: Glean credibility through the masses.
- Appeal to the customer and partnership base because we're born with a hostess mentality: Consciously and conscientiously leverage it to build respect and solidify your position as a power player.

During it all ... DO GOOD! For the company, for your team, for your peers, for your boss and for yourself — because that is what will make it all ... "glamorous."

Your Loving Mother,

Heidi Wissmiller
Chief Operating Officer
Rodan + Fields

Part Two

Create Balance

"You can't get second things by putting them first. You get second things by putting first things first."

~ C.S. Lewis

4

The Juggling Act

"Whatever is worth doing at all is worth doing well."
~ Lord Chesterfield

by Lisa

1998. Springtime in New York City. It was a glorious time to be on a weekend getaway with my husband, Ed, and some close friends. The city was in full bloom, and so was my career. After years of climbing the corporate ladder, at times putting in 60 or more hours a week, I had reached the rank of CEO. After being told we could never have children, we had a beautiful, healthy 4-year-old boy. Life was full, busy and, if I'm being honest, not completely balanced — but good.

Sitting in a darkened theatre on Broadway, we were absorbed in the heart-wrenching saga of *Miss Saigon*. A powerful scene showed a sea of Amerasian orphans left behind after the Vietnam War. I remember so clearly that moment, when my husband and I turned to look at each other … we just knew. God was not sending a subtle message; He was flashing a bright, green "go" light.

We had talked about adoption for years but set it aside after the birth of our biological son. We came home from NYC and started what we were told would be a three-year adoption process. Within six months, we were bringing home a little boy from a Russian orphanage who was deaf and mute and had a cleft palate.

It was time to practice what I preached about priorities. It was time to press "pause." It was time to downgrade my high-powered career to "plastic ball" status. Let me explain.

The Juggler

Many working women, especially mothers, would agree their lives often resemble a three-ring circus. At any given time, we could be flanked by a high-flying trapeze act in one ring and daredevil stunts in another, but in the third ring stands Mom. Mom is the juggler. Three, four, maybe six or more balls are being tossed into the air. Some soar high; others stay close.

It didn't happen overnight, of course. We may have started by learning to juggle a career and a spouse. Maybe we went back to school or took on a big volunteer project. Over time, we may have added one or many children. Then all of their activities. There is our faith, our home, our friends, our sanity. Is there room for an exercise ball? A "good nutrition and healthy meals" ball? There seems to be no end to the number of balls we are trying to keep in the air. The effort required to keep them all moving is relentless and exhausting. You may feel that if even one ball drops, you will be thrown off balance and the whole act will come crashing down. No! No! No!

Let go of that notion. You will achieve the holy grail of "a balanced life" only if you accept that some of those balls *can* and *should* drop, at least for a season. That is much easier to see if you know your priorities.

When we speak to groups of driven, high-achieving, and maxed-out working women, we tell them they are juggling five types of balls and challenge them to set their priorities according to the value of the ball and its importance in their lives.

The Five Balls

Crystal balls. Made of Waterford crystal, if you like, these are the most important balls in your life. If one drops, it shatters, and it will require an immense effort and a fair amount of heartache to try to piece it back together. Protect these balls fiercely. For me, my faith, my family and my closest friends are my crystal balls. I regret to say that for many years I made my career a crystal ball. But when that was the case, I never found the balance or fulfillment I was seeking.

Glass balls. These are key areas of our lives that are important to us but a step below the crystal balls. They can also shatter and break if dropped, but are generally replaceable or repairable with some time and effort. Work and volunteering are now my glass balls. I value them and do my best to keep them in the air.

Rubber balls. These are the things we manage on a routine basis, but in the grand scheme of things, they really do not matter quite as much as we think. You drop one and it bounces right back to you — just where you left off. Sometimes you may not even notice it dropped because it bounces back so quickly, and with little or no effort. The cleanliness and orderliness of my home at any given moment is a rubber ball. Throwing the perfect dinner party or the best 3-year-old birthday party ever, complete with a homemade cake and Pinterest-worthy decorations and party favors, could also be rubber balls. These are things you want to do or will do, but you probably need to ease up on the stress-inducing expectations of making everything perfect. These can become significant time-consumers if you aren't careful. Remember, these balls are rubber. They won't break. It's OK.

Plastic balls. These are areas of your life that you like — ones you try to keep in the air. But deep down you know they are not at the top of your priority list. Judge if you will, but fitness and healthy eating fell into this category for me for years. Now that I am an empty-nester with a little more time, they're a bit more important. Healthy family meals and at least 30 minutes of exercise a day are now habits. In years past, if those balls dropped for a time, no lasting havoc ensued. In fact, I find that when I drop a plastic ball it just sits there. It doesn't break; it doesn't bounce back; it doesn't even roll away. It just sits … waiting for the time when I can pick it up again and put it back into my routine. As I said, there was a time, after we adopted our son, when I knew that what I needed to do was tend to him and his needs, and my career became a plastic ball. I set it down. That's exactly where it needed to be for awhile.

Lead balls. These are the balls we need to drop and never pick up again. You may think you aren't trying to juggle lead balls, but we bet you are. For working women, false guilt and worry are almost always at the top of this list. Sometimes guilt and worry are justified. But I'm talking about the false guilt that comes with second-guessing yourself or caring too much about what others think or saying "yes" too often. False guilt is the type of guilt that we allow someone to place on us, as opposed to guilt from doing something we know is wrong. And we know the difference. We will talk more about this later. Over-obligation is also a lead ball. We say "yes" so we don't feel guilty — when we need to recognize that saying "no" opens doors for us to say "yes" to our crystal and glass balls. Draining relationships are another lead ball. Just as we have friends who rejuvenate and refresh us, there are others who drain us. Pay attention to the amount of time you spend with the latter; it affects your ability to feel balance and control in your life.

Crystal balls should remain crystal because they are the foundation of who we are. Other balls may change with the seasons of our lives. For instance, volunteering has become a glass ball for me; when I was busy raising children, it was plastic or rubber. My career has gone from crystal to plastic to glass. For every time there is a season, and seasons change. It's part of what makes life interesting and beautiful.

To-Do (or Not-To-Do) Lists

To-do lists are a time-honored tradition for working women. Without them we might feel like *Alice in Wonderland*, flailing down a rabbit hole. They allow us to be productive and keep us balanced and feeling in control. Right? Maybe. They might be controlling us instead. Maybe our lists are robbing us of spending quality time with those most important to us or leaving us feeling empty and "not enough" inside. If your to-do list leaves you with that feeling, throw it in the trash right now and start over.

While we can see the insanity of a pages-long to-do list for our friends or colleagues, we have somehow come to believe that it is OK for our own lists to go on and on. We have convinced ourselves that everything on them is necessary and worthwhile. Paula and I are just as guilty as anyone of falling into this trap.

I can remember a time when my to-do list, which I keep handy in my purse or on my desk at all times, was three pages long. This went on for days. I'm not just talking about a list of shopping items. These were legitimate — or so I thought at the time — things that needed to be done:

- finalize a big presentation (and practice it more than once)
- get a birthday card, cake and gift for my son
- get Mom a Mother's Day gift and one for my husband's Mom too
- pack for a business trip to two different climates
- return eight phone calls
- plan for a board meeting
- meet the new neighbors
- write five thank you notes

You get the idea. Unfortunately, this went on for days ... until truly, it was like a cloud hanging over my head. I had this constant sinking feeling knowing there was something that needed to be done and there just weren't enough hours in the day. It seemed like each time I crossed something off the list (yes, I am one of those people), I added two more. Talk about feeling not good enough.

I finally divvied up some of the items, scratched others off the list, and then created two lists. One was a more reasonable to-do list that traveled with me — my "crystal and glass ball items" — and the other was a longer-term list of things I wanted (and in some cases needed) to get done, but they could wait. Other things moved off my to-do list and onto my calendar a week or two before their due date. Making these visual breaks in my lists allowed sunlight to break through the clouds. It was easier to breathe ... and smile. Perfectionists sometimes put projects before people.

Ask yourself whether your to-do list represents your priorities. Go through your list and determine which type of ball each item is. Things will start to become "crystal" clear. When faced with one more thing that absolutely MUST be done TODAY, ask yourself, "Will this matter tomorrow?" If so, you may need to find a way to juggle it into your schedule, ideally replacing something else. If not, and usually it's not, the answer is simple — and you have more time to do the things that matter.

> *"Breaking up with perfect is hard to do, but what we gain is infinitely superior to what we give up."*
> — Amy Carroll

Do you spend your days reacting to the everyday urgencies of life? It might help to jot "stop and smell the roses" on your to-do list. It may seem silly, and roses may not even be in bloom, but adding an item that reminds you to slow down and find a pleasurable moment could also remind you to keep things in perspective. Because ladies, if you are too busy to have a little fun, you are TOO BUSY.

Multitasking

We are not here to debate the advantages and disadvantages of multitasking, but we must acknowledge its reality in the life of a busy woman — well, actually, in the lives of most people. Yes, we know research shows multitasking can actually decrease productivity and add stress. So we'll talk about how we use what we call "compatible multitasking" to help gain control of a busy day and leave us feeling more instead of less balanced.

For instance, I like to pray while walking. I find it a great way to start my day, both spiritually and physically. I look for ways to combine tasks that can be compatible and don't interfere with each other. I don't combine an important conversation with one of my sons and an important report for work. However, calling a parent or friend while I'm doing laundry or the dishes works well. As a matter of fact, I like supplementing a monotonous task with a chat — it makes the time go by faster. It also allows me to keep in touch with a few folks I might not otherwise talk to as frequently.

Today's technology allows us to be in two places at once, sort of. Paula recalls being out of town when her son had his first orthodontist appointment and calling into the office consultation by phone. At the time, the doctor's office thought that was odd, but these days with mobile phones, FaceTime and Skype, such behavior is commonplace and, let's face it, helpful. How often have we started a conference call at work and continued it through our commute home? The key is not to allow our multitasking to create more stress or become unhealthy.

Managing Murphy

Murphy is never invited to our home or office, yet has come to be expected. Sometimes Murphy merely does a drive-by and leaves as quickly as he came. Other times, usually our busiest times, Murphy stays for an extended visit.

We are talking, of course, about Murphy's Law. If something can go wrong, it will. For instance, the air conditioner doesn't break when it is 60 degrees outside — it breaks when it's 92. Or the gas grill is plenty full — until guests are arriving in 10 minutes for a party. Or how about this: The night before you have a 6 a.m. flight to see a client for a huge presentation, you get out the suit you bought for this all-important meeting, and it — what are the odds — still has the store alarm sensor attached to the skirt. *"Really?"* you ask. Yes!

Sound familiar? Well, we've discovered that these are simply the crazy things of life. Often, they come in threes … just because. While many of these circumstances are out of our control, the way we respond to them is not.

We can learn to laugh at life's annoyances, vent and get over them, or confide in a friend, someone who will listen without judging. Sometimes simply verbalizing your frustration can help you gain perspective on the situation. For others, writing down life's unexpected mishaps helps, even if you shred the paper later.

Holding onto our anger and annoyances, on the other hand, can lead to a bitter attitude that will not only steal our joy but make those around us pretty miserable, too. A sure-fire way to torpedo any feeling of fulfillment. We have found that practicing self-compassion is the best way to manage Murphy. If you treat yourself with the same compassion you would treat a friend, you will adapt better to life's hiccups and keep all the balls from crashing down.

Challenge Yourself

It's a daily challenge to set our priorities and live our lives according to them, but if we don't, the tyranny of the urgent will take control of our days. Our perspective on what matters most will become distorted, and the balance we are seeking will remain beyond our grasp. Society bombards us with information that confuses our priorities or misleads us into thinking and feeling as if EVERYTHING is a top priority, from ageless skin to being the top sales producer every month.

Don't be fooled or seduced by false guilt. If you devote your time and energy to your top priorities and take the time to *Remember Who You Are* when setting your priorities, your days will feel more balanced and you will actually be more productive. Whether your balls are in the air or on the ground, you will have mastered the art of juggling.

Dear Young Jenn,

The old saying "if I knew then what I know now" means so much more than what you are able to realize at this point in your life. That is the beauty of being young. You are not jaded by the experience of life, and you are full of energy and excitement about the uncertainty of what is ahead.

You spend your youth being naïve to reality. Being asked to go to the middle school dance and making the cheerleading squad are all that seem to matter. You take your parents for granted as they work hard to provide you with everything you could ever want, sitting through countless ballgames and dance recitals, cheering you on every step of the way. You become a teenager and think your parents are total idiots, and you pass judgement on their every move. Clearly no family could be anymore dysfunctional than your own. It becomes obvious later that you actually had a functional family compared with others.

You work hard to get good grades and high scores on your college placement exams so you can get into a good college. You rush through college so you can land a fabulous job at a fabulous company and move out on your own. After just a few years of living on your own, you find the person who will become the love of your life, and you get engaged, then married, and buy your first house in a lovely golf course community. Following the American norm, you get pregnant after exactly three years of marriage. You have a perfect little boy, and just two years later you are pregnant with a sweet little girl.

Then life starts to move fast, and you have no idea it is happening. You are in survival mode. The infant years seem like they will last forever. Sleep becomes overrated, but you still manage to get to work after dropping the kids off at daycare so you can keep that fabulous job at that fabulous company and pay for that fabulous home in that golf course community. Some days you may leave the house wearing mismatched shoes, or you may have forgotten to put on deodorant, but you get there on time, an accomplishment in itself.

Somehow those mismatched shoes and lack of deodorant land you a promotion at the top of your field at that fabulous company. For the first time you will doubt yourself and your ability. What if you fail? You will feel guilt for not always being able to balance it all. Your daughter's face when you arrive 15 minutes late for the dance recital because you were in a meeting will haunt you forever. The day you send your first child off to college will feel like a part of your soul has moved away. How could they ever live without you? And just four months after your son goes off to college, your father at 70 years young will die of a massive heart attack, throwing you the first real unexpected loss of your life. Your mother, whom you have watched your entire life be the rock and provider in the family, will now need you for strength and support.

If that all reads at the speed of the disclaimers at the end of a drug commercial, you get the point. Life blows by, and if you are not careful it will happen "to you" instead of "with you." You will regret the time you did not spend with your family and friends and regret the time you spent on things that you realize later are not important.

So here are just a few lessons to share as "I know now what I didn't know then."

1.   Do not let your job define you. Work hard and do something you love, but remember, it is just a job.

2.   Always put family first. You will never regret it.

3.   If you marry, remember: Forever is a long time, and it will not always be easy. The secret to a lasting marriage is to fall in and out of love over and over again (with the same person ☺).

4.   Be healthy. Without your health none of the rest matters.

5.   Don't spend more than you make, and always give some to others.

6.   Don't let self-doubt prevent you from trying something new. Women tend to doubt their abilities more than men, so man up!

7.   Always have a circle of female friends to lean on and be there for. Life gets busy, but at some point they will need you and you will need them, so don't neglect those friendships.

8.   Find a creative outlet or hobby to nurture your spirit.

9.   Get a good night's sleep.

10. If you are going to do it, do it really well.

Slow down, be present and enjoy the journey.

Older Jenn

Jenn Mann
Executive Vice President & Chief Human Resources Officer
SAS

5

Calendar Jam

"Wherever you are, be all there."
~ Jim Elliot

by Lisa

Swan's Point, Washington, NC. 1977. Nothing could be finer than to be in Carolina, sailing across the sound on a lazy summer day with the sun beaming down and the wind lifting your cares away. As a teenager, my beau-turned-husband would pick me up on Saturdays and whisk me down Highway 17 to the water's edge. He was the captain and I was his first mate on a tiny Sunfish. We settled into a comfortable division of duties worth the reward — hours of carefree sailing while we sang along with the soulful sounds of the Commodores.

Fast forward 25 years — married, two kids, two careers, working long hours yet trying desperately to keep all the balls in the air. We still love the water. Our time on the water has provided many hours of fun for our family; it is important to us. We often made plans to take the kids to the lake on Friday afternoons, but of course, it's rarely that easy. A client needs attention, a meeting runs late — there is no time to run home and change into lake attire. I phone Ed.

"Can you knock off a little early, pack the car and grab the boys? I'll meet you out there," was a common mayday call.

So that's what we did. I raced to the lake straight from work, stepping aboard in my business suit. And guess who I see across the water on her boat, with her family, in her business suit? Paula! When we say we feel as if we have lived parallel lives in many ways, we aren't kidding.

We know this is the life of many of our peers. If you asked a working mom to describe her typical day, it might go something like this:

5:30-6:30 a.m.: Wake up and get yourself ready. Maybe you exercise (wow, you ARE Superwoman), pray/meditate, check email, read the news, sip coffee/tea. Or not.

6:30-7:30 a.m.: Wake up kids. While they get ready, put on your makeup. Maybe you make breakfast. Maybe they fend for themselves. Maybe lunches are packed. Maybe they aren't. Figure it out.

7:30 a.m.: Scramble to get kids out the door, into the car or to the bus stop. Often there are multiple schools and multiple bus stops. You hope you didn't forget lunch.

8-8:30 a.m.: Arrive at the office in time for a business meeting. Put in a full day of 15-minute, 30-minute or 60-minute meetings, including a lunch appointment.

5:30-6 p.m.: Rush to wherever the kids are because that is where you want to be. Start a carpool. Finish a carpool. Do whatever mom duties are called for.

6-7 p.m.: Have dinner. Maybe you started the crockpot at 7 a.m., you have a meal kit ready to eat, or your spouse has pulled on the oven mitts. Maybe you grab something on the go.

7-9 p.m.: Check on homework status, do the bedtime dance (bath, read, etc.) and kiss the kids goodnight. Or maybe you are just sitting down to dinner. It happens.

9 p.m.: Catch up on emails, work projects, housework, school paperwork, laundry; you know this list goes on and on.

Midnight-ish: Go to bed so you can start over in six or so hours.

Whew! Have you ever written down everything you do in a day? We know some amount of crazy is part of the deal, and we accept that. If you are standing at the edge of the swimming pool cheering on your child with your toddler precariously perched on your hip, while you're wearing a business suit and heels (like Paula) — it's OK. In fact, give yourself a big high five for being there to see your child reach the finish line. But also realize that the inevitable *Calendar Jam* — a son's soccer game on one side of town at 6 p.m., a daughter's basketball practice on the other side of town at 6:30 p.m., a client expecting to have dinner with you at 7:30 p.m. — cannot and should not become your norm. If you haven't figured it out yet, you soon will: We are NOT Superwomen (and were not meant to be); we can NOT do it all on our own (and were not meant to). If we keep pounding that square peg, we will splinter and become ineffective and broken on every front — home, work, relationships. During this busy season of our lives, we need some sort of routine that works for our family and maintains our sanity.

Build Your Team

Early in my career, I was recruited by a company in Atlanta that would have given me a huge promotion. Ed and I had agreed we would follow whichever of us had the best career path, so he was willing to make the move. While I was having the final interview with this great company, Ed interviewed with another company nearby. He, too, got a great offer — but for a position based in our home city, so we wouldn't need to move. What to do? Well, we stayed. We liked North Carolina, and Ed really wanted the job. In this instance, I didn't follow the money, I followed my heart. We were a team. Just as you build a successful team at work, it helps to build one at home if you expect to be able to manage your work-home worlds. Paula and I are blessed. We have husbands who support our careers.

Ed and I always knew that if we had children they would be a top priority, and that meant at least one of us needed to have some flexibility at all times. Paula and Greg agreed early on — while he was still in law school — that having a family would mean one of them needed to be able to work in a big firm but the other would need something more adaptable. They have stuck to that. Of course, this doesn't prevent *Calendar Jam*, but if we hope to create balance in our family's calendar, we need to start with balance (and agreement) in our marriage. Working as a team, with our family as the top priority, has helped us through more than one of life's challenging transitions.

While some are fortunate enough to have a spouse or close family member at home while Mom is at work, others use a daycare center or a long-term babysitter or a nanny, as crucial members of the team. You find the solution that works best for your family and make no apologies. The bottom line is, if you have someone you trust and someone who shares your values to help you fill in the gaps, the sometimes overwhelming task of managing a busy family calendar can be tackled with confidence, or at least steely determination.

Involve your kids. Just as spouses and caretakers are crucial team members, so are your children. There's no time like the present to get them involved in helping the home run smoothly. From the time my boys were in elementary school, they were responsible for packing their own lunches and making their own beds. Everyone is expected to do their part because that is how families (and businesses) work best. To keep my sanity, we had house rules — keep your dirty shoes in the garage when you've been out playing in the woods; finish your homework before TV and video games. Not only was structure necessary to avoid chaos, but it also helped our children develop self-discipline and (some) time management skills. I consider that a win-win.

Delegate. No need to reinvent the wheel here. Divide and conquer wherever you can. Ask yourself: *Can we hire someone to clean the house on occasion, or even frequently?* (Bonus if they will do laundry because who doesn't hate laundry? That's also a good task to teach your children). *Can someone else take the clients to dinner? Can we carpool? Can we order groceries online?* Again, we think we need to do it all ourselves, but if you take a critical look at everything that needs to be done weekly, I bet you can find a way to move some things off your plate.

Set Boundaries

In addition to the house rules, we enforced a "one-sport-a-season" rule per child. Yes, there was the occasional overlap, but we quickly realized we could not spend every evening and weekend running from one activity to another. Many parents are so afraid of their child being left out or not "keeping up" that they sign them up to do anything and everything. Paula says she was guilty of taking on too many activities at times because she and Greg wanted to give their kids as many experiences as they could.

The problem is we all end up overscheduled and stressed out. In his book *The Over-scheduled Child*, child and adolescent psychologist Alvin

Rosenfeld talks about how a full calendar intended to enrich and instill confidence can actually cause depression, anxiety and a lack of creativity and problem-solving skills in our children. If you are struggling to figure out what should stay and what can go, Rosenfeld suggests, "First, I'd ask myself what kind of adult you want your kid to grow up to be. And then I'd ask how you get there. How do you balance academics, athletics and character?" If you really want to push yourself, don't just think about the answer; write it down. Seeing it in black and white might give you a perspective you hadn't considered. Asking your child what he/she prefers might also yield some surprising and insightful answers.

Paula found she had to set similar boundaries at the office to keep Calendar Jam at bay. She tells this story:

> *Alice had developed a habit of coming into my office to ask for approval for some documents right before the end of the day. She routinely expected others would drop everything to meet a deadline she had promised. I could have stayed until 8 p.m. to review the documents, but I put my foot down and said, "You can't bring this to me at this hour and expect me to drop everything professionally and personally to meet YOUR deadline." It should have been done earlier, and she needed to learn to respect my time. It was a harsh lesson, but I needed to set those boundaries to protect my time with my family.*

Adhering to the old adage, "Poor planning on your part does not constitute an emergency on my part," is absolutely necessary if you don't want someone else's calendar imposed on you. In fact, when planning our workdays, we have found it critical to block off time for ourselves to think ... and to go to the ladies' room. You laugh, but how many times have you gotten to the office and found yourself running from one meeting to the next, and before you know it it's 3 p.m. and you haven't had a break? Paula's assistant used to joke about needing to schedule bio breaks, just to make sure. That's an important task — calendar it!

Feeling unprepared in just one executive meeting was enough to tell Paula that she had to gain better control of her calendar. Instead of allowing herself to be booked in back-to-back meetings all day, all week, all month, she had her assistant schedule her one hour of "think time" every day. It was sacred time, and it had to be on the calendar. She could use it to return calls or emails or think about strategy and develop content for those important executive meetings.

You must constantly fight for yourself because there will always be someone or something trying to take that time from you. But trying to squeeze in one more thing — being late, unprepared, and stressed — is just not worth it. Create some margin for yourself — you and those around you will benefit.

There's a difference between being busy and being productive. We can all be busy all day long. But we want a calendar that helps us to be productive. At the end of the week, can you see what you accomplished? Do you find yourself in unnecessary meetings, or do they align with your strategic goals? If you are scratching your head at the end of the quarter and wonder why you haven't made more progress reaching your goals, take a hard look at your daily calendar and be willing to set limits — and say "no" when you need to.

Me Time

Not long ago, Paula and I stole away for a quick girls' beach getaway in the middle of the week. The sand in our toes, the wind in our hair, a full box of Sanders dark chocolate sea salt caramels and a good friend to laugh with. It felt downright decadent! But I was surprised when Paula confided it was her first girls' escape since college. What??? Yes, it happens. You are focused on your career, and you are focused on your family. You make choices.

Please, take it from us: Be conscious of your choices. With all those balls in the air and to-do lists piling up, Paula had done what most of us have done at one time or another — put herself at the bottom of the list, or worse, not on the list at all. To be fair to my good friend here, this was a conscious choice for her. She too, had to juggle things, and she chose to make time away with friends a plastic ball during that season of her life. She traveled enough for business, so it really became an easy choice for her. Now that her work schedule isn't quite so hectic, she can add getaways back to her routine. And I think she will, because we had fun!

Many of us have given up hobbies, weekend getaways and social clubs so we can put everyone else's needs first. Paula will tell you that for many years she sacrificed making good, true friendships because she just didn't give it the time. (Thank goodness she has rectified that!) Book club? Who has time to read a book for pleasure every month? Bunco? The neighborhood girls didn't even invite us because they assumed we were too busy. With hectic travel schedules and young families maybe we were, but it would have been nice to be asked.

Paula remembers tearfully telling a neighbor one night how hurtful it was not to be included. We all want to be included. We all need a break. But it is up to us to make, nay, take, time for ourselves to enjoy life's little pleasures. Your husband, children, boss, and co-workers will thank you for taking the time to recharge — it will reduce your stress and make you more productive, not to mention more pleasant to be around. The practice of self-kindness makes you kinder to others. Your world will immediately become brighter.

Different people rejuvenate themselves in different ways. Paula likes to work in the garden or be on the water. I like to shop, read and exercise. And being on the water is a bonus.

For me, recharging also means unplugging — sometimes altogether. No laptop AND no cellphone. I know this can't happen every weekend, and be prepared — it will be unsettling at first. Many of us can't even make it through a meal without checking our messages, let alone a weekend or a whole week. But trust us, you need to try it once or twice a year. Try spending a weekend without being connected. You could start by disconnecting for just one day of the weekend or even a few hours a week. It might take multiple tries, and this is understandable.

The dopamine release that happens in your brain every time a text pops up is very real. It makes us feel needed and cared for, but it is also a distraction and puts us in a constant state of multitasking, not a very conducive way to recharge.

The truth is, the connections that are the most fulfilling come in the real world, not the virtual world. Deep down, we know this. When you unplug and take "me time," your business emergencies will wait. In fact, we have found that by doing this — and yes, I "log off" from work emails from Saturday afternoon to Sunday evening many weekends — we have trained others to expect it, learn to make decisions on their own and recognize a "real emergency" when it happens. When you take time for yourself, you are also demonstrating great leadership. You are setting a good example for your employees to follow, which will make them more productive at work, too.

We know that taking luxurious vacations is not always possible, but ladies, who among us can't find time for even a little luxury — a long bath without interruption (scheduled when the kids are gone), a cozy chair with a good book, or a mani-pedi with a friend? It doesn't matter what you do; it only matters that you do it. And you can't say you'll do it when you "have time" because that time will never come. Let us repeat this: There is nothing wrong with pampering yourself. Take a few moments to think about what refreshes you, what relaxes you, then carve out a little time each week to treat yourself. It can make a world of difference.

Gut Check

Even with all your perfectly prioritized to-do lists, your color-coded calendars, and your meticulous attention to detail, never dismiss your gut instinct. Be willing to toss the whole plan out the window if you see one of your breakable balls coming down. As a mother, you know when something is amiss academically, socially, or medically. As our children mature, we have to be prepared to respond, even if that means ditching the nanny so one parent can spend more time at home.

Paula and I have both had seasons of our lives when this was necessary. We have to remain flexible. The calendar is meant to help us manage our home and work lives so we can better deal with unpredictabilities and feel more balanced and fulfilled. If that isn't happening, I know it's time to grab my husband and head for the water.

Dear Iris,

What is most important in your life? Health? Family? Career? Adventure? Whatever your priority, there is probably a single underlying theme: Time. Time is our most precious good, which is inevitably running and our remaining time becomes shorter with every day.

As a consequence, it should be natural that we all want to spend time on our priorities. And what is your reality? How much time do you invest every day in what matters most to you? Let me guess: only a small portion. Your day is filled with meetings, one-on-one or in groups; calls, often with several bookings in parallel, and no time to prepare and debrief properly; and then there are the 100 e-mails every day and the business trips, domestic and cross-continental. And the worst consequence of this avalanche of activities is that you do not even have time to think about the dilemma. Actually, you might not even realize that you are living a dilemma because you feel how important you are – you drive meaningful projects, resolve issues, manage people; you perform extraordinarily well. The avalanche also covers all your hidden wishes, your dreams, concerns and regrets because you continue to risk missing important milestones in the lives of the people you love: your little daughters' first words, their school theater performances, your partner's latest success.

Life is about making choices. Not taking a decision is a choice, too, and will create its own consequences. So, start making your deliberate choices about how you spend your time. Just be honest with yourself: There is no way that you can please everybody and that you can satisfy all demands on you. Once you realize this, you will gain the new freedom to prioritize and to be transparent about these decisions.

Look at your calendar – business and family – of the next month and decide which business activities will create the most value and which are there because they always have been. Focus with visible consistency on the important, valuable commitments and excuse yourself from the others. You will find that the world is not falling apart because you are not at certain meetings. Your importance will not diminish. If anything, by focusing on what matters and delivering swiftly on business imperatives, your contribution will become more visible and appreciated. To maximize the opportunity, you do not only free up your time by removing low-value activities. Your business environment could benefit from a thorough "task" vs. "value" analysis and removal of the "task only" commitments. Doesn't that sound great? You have the courage and you create win-wins.

Work from the assumption that weekends should be free for family and leisure time. The rule will require occasional exceptions, and that should be manageable as business and personal life become increasingly intertwined through mobile technologies. However, the starting point should be the weekend as a fixed point to relax and recover – and that's good for business, too, because you will be fitter and happier when the next week starts. The purpose of the weekend is not that you finish the overflow of work to be ready for the next week. By better planning and managing your business days, you will have less unfinished business.

The next challenge is to not allow your calendar to fill up quickly again. Focusing on what matters most is a constant battle; however, it should become the strategy of your life. Be decisive about what matters and, as a result, about how you spend your time, the most precious good in your life. Everybody can keep herself busy – the art is about being in charge of the choices. Enjoy the new freedom!

With warm regards,
Iris

Prof. Dr. med Iris Loew-Friedrich
Chief Medical Officer
Executive Vice-President Development and Medical Practices
UCB S.A.

6

Conquering Guilt and Worry

"I cannot give you the formula for success, but I can give you the formula for failure — try to please everybody."
~ Herbert Bayard Swope

by Paula

Houston, Texas, September 1996. Dinner, drinks and good conversation flowed at a swanky downtown restaurant. I was on the verge of landing a $20 million deal I had worked hard to prepare for, and quite frankly, I was feeling pretty good about myself. But when I got back to the high-rise hotel and turned on the TV, that feeling immediately turned to panic, worry and guilt. Images of devastation flashed across the screen; a deadly Category 3 hurricane had slammed into the North Carolina coastline and moved inland right through my community.

I was 1,200 miles from my young family with no way of getting in touch with them. All the phone lines were down, and all the flights into Raleigh were canceled. I managed to get a flight to Charlotte, where I rented a car and started an agonizing three-hour drive home. Mile after mile I drove, seeing the devastation Hurricane Fran had wrought — downed trees and demolished cars and homes. When I arrived at my own home and was stopped by a 100-year-old tree across the driveway, I was near tears. Thank goodness, my husband and 1-year-old baby girl were all right, but I was a wreck!

Why had I gone? I knew a hurricane was churning in the Atlantic. *Was the meeting that important? Who was more important?* It was my husband's birthday, for crying out loud. The questions in my mind were unrelenting. I beat myself up for days, months, possibly years. The working mom's biggest nemesis — guilt — was raging inside me.

Just seven years earlier I had turned down an offer to continue working in Europe — a decision I was told could derail my career — because I wanted to come home and give the courtship with my future husband a real chance. Naturally, I had met this handsome rock star after I had accepted an overseas assignment (and sworn off men). We racked up a $7,000 transatlantic phone bill that first year paying by the minute, which was a third of my annual paycheck!

Now, after the storm, I wondered if my compass was off, if my priorities were straight, if putting my career before my family, in this instance, was a sign that I had failed as a wife and mother.

I share this very personal story because I learned some valuable lessons that have helped me deal with guilt in both the short and long term. In the short term, I can tell you it caused me to prepare better for the *what-ifs* before I leave town. *What if* I don't get home on time? *What if* something happens at home? *What if* something happens to me? In this situation, as in most things, I learned that preparation is a good antidote to guilt. If you spend time preparing — whether for a presentation at work or for your family in your absence — you spend less time feeling guilty about the outcome. Today, my husband and I can laugh about the fact he thought a box of ice cream sandwiches and a six-pack of beer were adequate hurricane provisions, but I promise you that, at the time, not stocking the refrigerator and pantry before I left was another source of guilt.

In the long term, I learned to evaluate guilt to help determine how I would let it affect me. Life coach, author, and dear friend Debbie Wilson introduced us to the idea of **false guilt**. False guilt comes from things over which we have no control — hurricanes, for instance. Or it's guilt that is placed on us by someone else — "*I am so sorry your husband can't support your family and that you had to go back to work*" (yes, someone actually said this to Lisa after the birth of their first son and yes, her husband was capable of supporting their family). Or it's guilt that comes as a result of not meeting standards or expectations that were handed down to us or even created by us — "*Did you use Mama's scratch recipe for Johnny's birthday cake or buy it at the grocery store?*" Honestly, the list of things we can allow ourselves to feel guilty about is never-ending. When a British survey found that 96 percent of women feel guilty at least once a day and 50 percent up to four times a day, a new moniker for today's women emerged: the Guilty All the Time (GAT) generation. That doesn't seem too far off the mark in our country either.

True guilt, on the other hand, comes from knowing we have done something wrong or knowing we have made a decision that doesn't align with our priorities. First and foremost, we need to be clear about what our priorities are — priorities that ideally have been set in conjunction with our spouses if we are married. Knowing our priorities can not only protect us from false guilt when it creeps up but can help us learn from our mistakes and make appropriate changes if we are experiencing true guilt.

Today, I can honestly make these two statements about my trip to Houston: *I don't regret going. I regret not staying at home.* "But Paula," you might say, "those are conflicting statements." Yes … but they are both true. Of course, if I had the benefit of hindsight, I would have stayed home and sidestepped this guilt-ridden situation. However, acknowledging that I cannot possibly know everything that will happen allowed me to let go of the false guilt I had been feeling. But I had to break it down. Although we knew a storm was brewing, its predicted path when I left town was south of our state. My husband was completely supportive of my decision to go. We did not know what would happen, and we had no control over it.

So, back to my berating questions. *Why had I gone?* To secure a lucrative deal and partnership for my company, which was my job. My career allows me to provide for our family, which is something my husband and I both value. *Was the meeting that important?* Yes. Had we known a hurricane would hit, we could have re-scheduled, but that is information we didn't have at the time. *Who was more important?* My family. Period. No question.

I evaluated the situation. I reaffirmed my priorities. I prepared more for future trips. Now, it was time to put it behind me and move on. I just wish I had done it sooner.

Worry Lines

What woman would tell you she likes worry lines? None, of course, but that doesn't stop us from piling worry — anxiety and uncertainty over actual or potential problems — on top of guilt for a toxic little concoction that seems to poison hours of every day. Before we know it, the terrible twins of guilt and worry are driving forces that affect our lives in ways we would never consciously allow. Consider the effects of guilt and worry:

- increased stress
- decreased self-esteem
- fatigue
- extreme behaviors (too much drinking, food issues, etc.)
- unclear thinking and decision-making
- lack of needed discipline with our children (because we are tired and likely feeling guilty)

In her book *Give Yourself A Break*, Debbie reminds us that worry not only keeps us problem-focused, but over time it actually changes who we are. "It changes our character and our relationships. Today you are becoming the person you will be tomorrow," Debbie says.

It's true. We realized the way we handled guilt and worry not only affects how we perform and are perceived at work, it affects our children and how they react to us. They are very perceptive. If we worry, they worry. Who wants to look back on their life and think of the person they could have been if only they hadn't let guilt and worry shape their decisions and outlook? Not us. Taking a deep breath and recalling one of our favorite Bible verses is our favorite way to refocus and break free from the worry that can cause a fault line in our lives.

Do not be anxious about anything, but in every situation, by prayer and petition, with thanksgiving, present your requests to God. And the peace of God, which transcends all understanding, will guard your hearts and your minds in Christ Jesus.
— Philippians 4: 6-7 (NIV)

Pause.

Realistic Expectations

The meal was cooked; the table was set; my husband and children were ready to eat dinner. The only thing missing was … me. I said I would be home for dinner by 6 p.m., but something came up at the office and I didn't get home until 7 p.m. After a few times of this, my husband sat me down and told me bluntly not to promise something I couldn't deliver. I adhered to that standard at work; certainly my family deserved the same treatment. He was SO right. I hadn't realized how showing up late for dinner affected my family and stood to affect my children's ability to trust me. Cue the guilt train. I nipped that in the bud quickly. If I said I would be home for dinner by 6:30 p.m., I would do everything I could to get home by 6:15 p.m. I told them what to expect, and then I did my best to meet it or exceed it. I was rewarded with more smiles and less guilt.

We believe one of the first and most important things women need to do when it comes to expectations is give themselves permission to say "no." No, we don't have to do it all. No, we do not need to attend every sporting, musical or academic event in which our children participate. It's OK to be OK with that — it's OK not to feel guilty. Children are, for the most part, adaptable and resilient. If your son has eight soccer games, for instance, and you can put four on your calendar (you have just made this a priority), think of how happy he will be if you are able to show up for more than you promised. But if you promise you will come to every game and don't follow through, your children will lower their expectations of you. Not only are we setting a bad example for our children, we just bought another guilt trip.

Setting realistic expectations allows us to focus our energy on what we are doing instead of what we are missing. This takes a lot of practice, we know, since it seems to go against our hardwiring. But these are the things we do to manage guilt.

Creative Connections

When a six-week international executive program that I needed for my career advancement required me to spend three weeks in France and three weeks in Singapore, I knew I couldn't do it without my family. So we made the family part of the experience. We invested the money for them to visit me twice — once in France and once in Singapore — and they got their first taste of international travel. It also made the kids feel they were part of my work life, and it started us on a fun travel adventure project. I decided to start giving them my frequent flier miles. When I would travel, they would benefit with a cool trip and education. Soon it became a game — the miles would come in the mail, and they would get out the globe and start calculating where we could go. They helped plan a magical 17-day trip to Antarctica and an amazing trip to the Galapagos Islands.

Of course, trips don't need to be exotic, but allowing our children to benefit from our travel has been a way to help show them the value in what we do. Lisa would sometimes take one or both of her sons along with her. From her planned trips, they would get to choose a city or two that they most wanted to visit that year, and the family would find a way to make Mom's work travel fun for all of them.

One of the best things about being working mothers is that it has forced us to be creative in connecting with our kids. Because we were not home with them all the time, creating traditions and rituals took on even more importance, and helped keep guilt at bay. For instance, I made a point to take off work and chaperone as many school field trips as I could. If I knew I was going to have late nights at work, I would surprise them at school for lunch. My favorite time of the day when I was traveling was calling home at bedtime. My husband would put the phone on speaker (today it's FaceTime) between the bedrooms, and we would all pray together. It was a special time for us. We connected despite the distance. I miss those days.

Lisa created a reputation with her sons and their friends by putting a little note of encouragement or cartoon strip in their lunch boxes, even when she was traveling (she had them pre-cut). It's such a simple thing, but she kept it up through high school — and if she ever forgot a day, her son and his friends would demand to know what happened. They were all waiting to read what crazy cartoon Mrs. Grimes would tuck into the lunchbox.

Lisa also made it a tradition to take her children's birthdays off each year when they were young. That was a day her sons knew was theirs and theirs alone. A special breakfast complete with table decorations, cupcakes for the class on occasion, lunch at school, her car in carpool line, a visit from Nana and Papa C, and their chosen meal or dinner at their favorite restaurant. The point was she made a commitment to be home, not in NYC or LA, but with them on their birthdays. For working mothers, these special times are needed and cherished, and they make the tough times a little bit easier.

Speak Out

It is much easier to bandy about the "work-life balance" phrase than to come up with the formula that allows you to live it. Life is much too messy and fluid. Although books, conferences, and commencement speeches exhort today's young women to speak out, or, as Sheryl Sandberg would say, "lean in" and demand a workplace that allows them to be professionally successful and still committed to their families, the reality is, it's not that cut and dried. The good news is, it is a revolution we have been a part of and can help further.

Today, I would be much quicker to cancel a meeting for a family obligation or reschedule that trip to Houston. Lisa doesn't lose sleep over suggesting an alternate meeting date with a key client because she is going to be out of the office on the client's preferred date (because she has vacation plans). Discretion and good judgment will always be critical if you want to remain effective in business but also honor family obligations. We realize we are older, we hope wiser, and more confident, and we have already made it to the executive ranks. I remember well the feeling I had on my climb, that I had to work harder than my male counterparts and show impenetrable strength to advance. I absolutely believed that if I spoke too much about family obligations or bowed out early too often, that would be perceived as weakness. No, I can say with certainty it would have been perceived as weakness because I watched other women's careers veer off track for similar offenses. Sandberg and Anne-Marie Slaughter, among others, have written on this topic, and we agree this is likely to change as more women reach the tops of their industries.

But therein lies the chicken and egg question. Can you truly have a healthy work-life balance as you climb? Or can you achieve work-life balance only *after* you make it to the top, if at all? Current sentiment suggests the latter for women in executive roles. So, how to swing that pendulum so more women make it to the top? We don't have all the answers, but we know that women supporting women is a good start, and breaking out of the vicious guilt cycle is critical.

So, this is our advice:
- Establish your credibility.
- Be the team member who delivers X plus (remember, this does not always mean working the most hours).
- Operate from a place of courage and confidence — not guilt — and don't be shy about telling your boss or subordinates when you have a family priority. Just remember to offer the condensed version.

If we are not constantly making excuses for missed deadlines, we will actually be more respected when we choose to put non-work priorities first. We will also be setting a good example for other women of what balance looks like, and contributing to acceptance of balance in the workplace, for men and for women. This does not mean we turn the boardroom into a confessional. Everyone does not need to know every detail about every appointment in our calendar. In fact, when we give too much information and come across as apologetic or seeking affirmation, we are allowing guilt to drive us. Why? Let's stop that.

Take a page from the male playbook. Men don't say they need to bug out of a meeting early to make the noon pickup game in the gym. They just say, "I have an appointment." Women can do the same. Or, they can stand up with confidence and without guilt and say, "I have a hard stop at 11:30 a.m. I'm having lunch with my son." Either works — you have to be the judge of what is appropriate and when.

We are not going to tell you that you can or can't have it all, because what constitutes "all" is different for each of us, and it changes with the seasons of our lives. But if you are making decisions with your priorities in mind and not out of a sense of guilt, you are more likely to feel that work-life seesaw is not hitting the ground.

The Big Picture

When that well-meaning older lady questioned Lisa about going back to work after having her son, it was like a stab in the heart. No mother wants to feel her choices are hurting her children. We all have examples of times when people have made insensitive comments that have inflicted guilt or caused us to question ourselves. It is up to us to own our choices and reject that false guilt. There is nothing wrong with asking yourself the tough questions and revisiting priorities with your spouse from time to time. There is nothing wrong with the balance shifting, during life's seasons, as you see fit. If it helps, write down all the reasons you have chosen to pursue your career. Focus on what you do well and all the benefits you provide your family and yourself. Not only was I the primary breadwinner in my family, but pursuing a challenging career bolstered me personally and gave me a sense of accomplishment.

Lisa and I both get a high by doing things well and feel we are at our best when we are challenged and learning. It's who we are.

Not that we need validation from the Harvard Business School, but all working women should rejoice in the findings of the "working mother effect" study conducted through Harvard's Gender Initiative. The global survey found that daughters with working mothers ended up performing better in the workplace, earning 23 percent more money and possessing more powerful positions than their peers with stay-at-home mothers. Sons of working mothers benefit, too.

"There is no single policy or practice that can eliminate gender gaps at work and at home. But being raised by a working mother appears to come very close to that," writes Harvard professor and author Kathleen McGinn. "Women raised by a working mother do better in the workplace, and men raised by a working mother contribute more at home."

In her seminal essay, *Why Women Still Can't Have It All*, Anne-Marie Slaughter introduced us to best-selling author Bronnie Ware. In her memoir, *The Top Five Regrets of the Dying*, Ware shares the regret she heard most often while interviewing the dying patients for whom she was caring: *"I wish I'd had the courage to live a life true to myself, not the life others expected of me."*

That, friends, is the big picture. *Remember Who You Are…* and don't feel guilty about it.

Dear younger self (at college graduation),

The massive number of grads taking their seats on the nearly filled football field will leave you feeling swallowed up. Such a paradox from your prior schooling of small class size, individual attention, regimented rules.

Shortly now ... dad will die. In an instant you will feel your heart ripped from your chest. You will be driven to your knees with a pain so excruciating, it will leave you feeling lifeless yourself. You will be forced to grow a spine of steel. Your dreams of med school will be shattered by financial impossibility far greater than the challenges of college that consumed you before. You will instantly become father to your younger siblings, and husband to your young 52-year-old mother. You will have no choice. You will become robotic, and you will execute.

Before you succumb to the desperation of the distraught, I want to stop you. These horrific next few years will be the launch pad for a life more blessed and wonderful than you have yet imagined.

It will all be fine ... better than fine. You will find the strength and courage to flourish. It is the struggle you are about to endure that will supply you with the drive to face a plethora of annual challenges. You have gathered enough tools of challenge in your tool belt to succeed, as now you'll create power tools. All of this has prepared you to adapt, address and advance.

You will find power in your stealth as no one expects your success.

This crisis will be the benchmark for battling through any future crisis. You will witness and lose family in a world changing terrorist event in this country. Further, capitalism will break, and you and your firm will have a ring side seat. Be reassured that you will find yourself, still standing and better for it.

Your heart will become that much softer. Guard it ... as that will truly become your Achilles' heel. You will discover the true definition of selflessness and empathy. You will not only fight the bully, you will reflexively defend others from him. It will be difficult, but hold your temper, always. You will become an advocate of inclusion. You will support and mentor without hesitation. One thought ... before you run into a burning building ... think first. Some people, some battles, may not be worthy of the effort.

You will not seek the spotlight as your goal. It will come on its own, if earned. Don't be driven by materialistic goals or people, lest they become your master.

Your focus on your career will pay off to where money is no longer a survival priority ... then to not a priority at all. You will not lose the house; your biggest fear. You will be family guardian for the rest of your life. The resentment fades as you will grow to relish the job. Your anger with God will end and you will grow even more spiritual.

I will not take away the excitement of your future and living many wonderful experiences. I'll just say you will marry and have a family that most people only dream about. Your children will have critical, frightening health moments where you will beg their lives are spared. In those times, your prayers will be answered. Your children will defy all odds, and excel. They will be bright and athletic. Mostly, they will be challenged and come up warriors, yet they will remain kind and compassionate.

By now, younger self, you realize that I'm telling you the road will be sometimes painful beyond words. Revel in the fact that the rough sea now is claiming you as its surrogate, but soon you will be its master. You will learn to trust your instincts.

No one will know your life better than you. Take advice but listen to your soul. Read the poem "If" by Kipling ... regularly. Remember that honesty, integrity and virtue have no gray areas.

Alan Turing said, "Sometimes it is the people no one imagines anything of who do the things that no one can imagine."

You will learn that it's great to have a plan and goals, but to not fight life's redirection. Take educated chances. Be brave.

Thank God for unanswered prayers. Above all, don't spend so much time on worry and fret, much of life's path is out of your control. Learn to "roll with it." You will sometimes have to make hard choices. You may have to move past others, but never step on another as you advance. Never let ego absorb you. Be fearful of those who do.

Hang on tight ... it's going to be a wild ride, but you will look back as I am now, appreciative of all the battles, enjoying the lessons and fruits of the labor, and holding dear all those who matter.

Above all ... love deeply, push the outside of the envelope, be a safe place for those who come after you seeking advice, and ... never forget where you came from.

With love,
Louise Armour

Financial Advisor
Managing Director
J.P. Morgan Securities LLC

Part Three

Experience Fulfillment

"Do all the good you can,
By all the means you can,
In all the ways you can,
In all the places you can,
At all the times you can,
To all the people you can,
As long as ever you can."
~ John Wesley

7

Complementing Beats Competing

"Strong people don't put others down … They lift them up."
~ Michael P. Watson

by Lisa

Sandbagged. My mid-twenties. My career was on the fast track, or so I thought. I had just received two promotions in short order at a Fortune 500 company. As a mid-level manager, I was managing other managers. I was making strong, steady progress up the proverbial corporate ladder. So when I got a call from the C-suite one day asking for a meeting with a top executive, I had no idea what it was about but I wasn't worried. When I walked into his office and saw a female executive sitting there — a woman who found a way to be critical of me more often than not — I knew there was trouble.

Sure enough, she had gone to the head of the company (instead of to me) and complained about something I had done. I was reprimanded in front of her, and I was forced to undo what I had done — something my boss had approved. It was embarrassing and humiliating. And eye-opening. Yes, I knew women could be catty, but that was the first real professional claw that had ever been sunk into me.

The snide comments, the rumors, the backbiting. Women who smile sweetly even as they work to sabotage other women, believing if they keep others down they will elevate themselves. Their *modus operandi* is to undermine with a million little cuts, a slowly twisting knife, a not-so-quiet whisper.

"Did you see what she was wearing?"

"Did you see that presentation she just gave? We have to help her."

"Bless her heart, she couldn't help being late for the meeting; she's got three kids at home."

The list of creative and unkind ways women compete with one another is shamefully long. Middle school and high school mean girls can morph into office mean girls. Or girls who were bullied by the mean girls in adolescence look to exact some sort of comeuppance when they achieve a measure of power in the workplace. Men are quick to point out, and sometimes exploit, this difference between the sexes. Whether we acknowledge it or not, female cattiness is a weakness that brings the whole sisterhood down. While men will compete with one another in the workplace and go out and have a beer later, competitive women tend to view one another as Public Enemy No. 1 for months, or years.

Women are Women's Worst Enemies

There is a growing body of research that contends this intrasexual competition does make a bit of sense. Tracy Vaillancourt, PhD, a Canadian researcher, asserts that women, in a primal instinct to be attractive to males, employ two basic competitive strategies in dealing with other women: self-promotion (which involves anything that makes them look more attractive to men) and the derogation of rivals by indirect or social aggression. Women prefer indirect aggression over direct aggression because it can harm other women in a "socially skilled manner" that prevents any physical harm to themselves or their children — a primal protective instinct. At its root, the competition among females is really a competition for mates. Consciously or not (we hope not), it carries over into every facet of modern life.

We are not willing to give the sisterhood a "pass" and simply call this backbiting culture a "survival of the fittest" competition. We advocate building a supportive network — of women, for women, by women. We understand that many women, maybe even you, have a real fear, an insecurity when it comes to other women. Maybe you are afraid that an idea may be stolen, or that you will be viewed as less intelligent than someone else. Maybe you fear that other women will be liked better by co-workers. Maybe you are envious of their appearance. Maybe you fear there is only room for one or two women at the top of your organization, so you feel you need to knock other women down so you are the only one left standing. We'll get to that issue in a minute, but you need to get past that fear and insecurity, consider your personal brand (what you want people to think of when they hear your name), and *Remember Who You Are.*

Mindful Change

So how can you train yourself to complement instead of compete? Well, I can tell you when I was in my twenties, I could have handled that choice better. When that woman sandbagged me, I was defensive. I engaged. I was quick to connect her to any perceived slights. Looking back, I should have asked her for an appointment and perhaps sought her out for some career coaching or advice. At a minimum, I should have tried to build a bridge and some sort of relationship instead of avoiding her and thinking she was always out to get me. There is no better way to disarm a competitor than to ask for help. This actually gives someone the space to compliment — and even complement — you as well. Building bridges, not burning them, is always the better way.

We have learned (and wish we had learned earlier) to be mindful of a few things that help keep us focused on complementing instead of competing.

Be vulnerable. Early on, I viewed vulnerability as a weakness. Now I view it as a strength. It doesn't come easy to me, and I don't think it does for most people, especially career women. We don't want to be seen as struggling. We don't want to share our shortcomings. We don't want to expose our flaws. We want to be seen as having it all together. The problem with that? NO ONE DOES. No one. When we work so hard to put up that front of perfection, we are preventing ourselves from being *real* and *transparent* and *approachable*. These are the things that allow us to connect with others on a deeper level, build trust and respect, achieve greater things for our companies and, yes, get that next promotion. Without it, we create an island for ourselves. A lonely island.

Later in her career, after having been burned by a few females herself, Paula embarked on a relationship with another senior-level woman in her company. This female executive was the head of a peer business team and was responsible for checking the quality of Paula's department.

Paula knew the relationship could easily become adversarial. Instead, she decided to enter into the relationship with the goal of complementing and not competing. When she was upfront and transparent with her colleague about her desire and willingness to work with her for the success of the company, the woman was cautiously receptive. Initially, they both had their guards up, but they worked to prove themselves to each other and eventually built a trust, and even a friendship. They would sometimes disagree, but with respect. They didn't use their disagreements as a way to tear each other down. But it had to start with *being real* and being willing to show a bit of vulnerability to foster a deeper connection.

Build your track record. Focus on doing *your* job well and don't worry about what others are or are not doing. Meet deadlines. Exceed expectations. Play by the rules. Your work will speak for itself. This not only establishes credibility among your peers, but once you have a string of successes under your belt you will feel better about showing a little vulnerability — and that can further your success. Doing your own good work will also lessen the temptation to undermine someone else's work. Trust us; someone — usually an executive — will eventually catch on to someone who is always criticizing and undercutting others' work.

Be confident. Yes, we are talking about confidence again. When you are confident in yourself — your abilities, your appearance, your relationships — you will be less likely to feel threatened by other women and less inclined to feel the need to put other women down. It's as simple as that. Confidence is a great antidote to cattiness. *You don't need to be perfect to be confident.* You don't even need to be where you want to end up. Confidence can come in just being on the right path and striving to be the best "you" that you can be. And the best "you" is not someone else. No need to dwell too long on what others might think of you; focus on your positives and own them – as well as owning your not-so-positives. Of course, there is always the danger of being too confident, to the point of being egotistical. That attitude is sure to put a bull's eye on your back and set you up for contentious relationships with women and men.

Invest in others. To paraphrase Aristotle, "Our whole is so much greater than the sum of our parts." It took us a while to learn this, but the little-practiced secret is that you are more likely to propel your own career and feel better about it if you help other women succeed in theirs. I wish I'd been coached earlier in my career to be a little less focused on my next promotion and more focused on helping those around me get theirs. I was so convinced I had to work harder and longer than everyone else to get ahead, I was laser-focused on my own path. I didn't intentionally step on colleagues, but I wasn't necessarily focused on others' careers either. I'm sure I left baggage along the way. I regret that. It took me a little while to learn firsthand that women investing in other women creates a culture that not only eliminates unhealthy competition and animosity but elevates everyone. It also sends a message to men that women can support other women.

In short, we must push beyond the fear. Instead of clawing our way over one another to the one or two top positions, let's focus on creating more top positions for more women and help one another get there.

The C-suite

The C-suite at Paula's company's world headquarters was the power center for the organization. The nucleus of a global conglomerate. At one time, the only women to occupy seats on the executive floor were the administrative assistants of the executive team … and Paula. Actually, even before she became a member of the executive team the company leaders gave her an office on the executive floor. The optics were better if at least one woman was on "the" floor.

To be a token representative is not the goal. Eventually, she became a company president, second to the CEO, managing 22,000 employees worldwide, and legitimately claimed her spot on the executive team. While she was very aware there were no female peers on the floor — no one to bounce ideas off of, no one to support or cheer on, no one to share the struggles of being an executive, wife and mother — she didn't realize right away what her presence on "the" floor meant to other women in her company. It took her colleague Elizabeth to point it out. Paula tells the story:

Elizabeth was more than 10 years my senior and several levels below me. She approached me in the cafeteria one day and waved her finger in my face. "You are our hope," she said. "All the women in the building look up to you because they see you got there." I left that conversation thinking: I have to do something. I have to let the women in our company know: The only thing between you and the C-suite … is you.

Even though I wasn't yet a member of the executive team, I left that conversation thinking: What next? About a month later I submitted a one-page proposal to the all-male executive team. I proposed that I gather an advisory committee of women and men to explore our culture for women aspiring to management positions. I explained that I didn't know what the effort would look like but that I knew what it would not look like. I explained that establishing quotas — a percentage of executive women — was not my intent.

I was given permission to proceed, and three months after Elizabeth waved her finger in my face, we were on our way to developing the Women Inspired Network (WIN). WIN continued for many years as an internal global organization for women to receive mentoring and to collaborate (not compete) with other women, to help build a culture for all women to grow and develop within the organization. Periodic speakers, book club discussions, and mentoring programs were available to all members. It improved the culture and morale for women, and men, too.

Europe has a different approach — establishing government quotas for women on corporate boards. Norway has set its quota at 40 percent, Germany at 30 percent and so on. The "30% Club" has branches in Britain and the United States to promote, though not mandate, 30 percent gender diversity on boards. However, a study led by Marianne Bertrand of the University of Chicago found that the European laws, while increasing female board percentages, did not result in greater numbers of females in executive positions, or decrease the gender pay gap or increase family-friendly policies — all worthy measures of true (vs. token) progress.

We do not believe in quotas. We believe women should serve on boards and in C-suites not simply because we are women, but because we are qualified and have earned the right to be there. We also believe women possess an intuition and emotional intelligence that can benefit companies and their boards. Where men tend to compartmentalize, women often connect the dots in a bigger picture and are able to see below the surface, into the hearts and minds, if you will, of the people we work with and the customers we serve. Executive men have said to us, "I really want a woman on my board because we need that perspective. We could use a fresh point of view." We agree.

In the United States, the 2020 Women on Boards organization has a goal of increasing the percentage of women on corporate boards to 20 percent by 2020. In 2016, its Gender Diversity Index of Fortune 1000 companies showed that 18.8 percent of corporate directors were women. When you consider that women compose about half of the U.S. workforce, hold half of all management positions and are responsible for almost 80 percent of all consumer spending, there is room and reason for those numbers to grow. The index also showed that more than 85 percent of companies with female CEOs or board chairs have already met or surpassed that board diversity goal — proof that women are helping women reach the top. This is something to cheer about and a great incentive to keep working to move the dial.

Research by Catalyst, a non-profit organization promoting women's issues in the workplace, adds more heft to the argument with evidence that increasing the number of women on boards leads to better financial performance of a company and greater charitable giving (corporate social responsibility).

What Happens When You Choose to Complement?

Simply put, lives change. Yes, the gender diversity numbers will go up. Yes, companies can be more successful. But you also make personal connections that speak to the core of who you are.

We have told you how Paula and I initially faced off as fierce competitors, always keeping our eye on each other, always gunning to lead the team that came out on top. I'm sure I would have said it wasn't personal, it was just my competitive nature. We can both say with certainty that when our relationship took a turn from competing to complementing, both our personal and professional lives improved.

In the last 15 years, since our first lunch date, we have both experienced a relationship that is not only more fun than keeping each other at arm's length, with a wary eye over each shoulder, but more fulfilling on all levels.

Once we established each other as "in-network," each of us immediately became a sounding board for the other. It's difficult to put a value on finding a person who can understand you personally and professionally. For us, there is not only an understanding and appreciation of what the other has been through, but a willingness to listen, disagree without fear, and ask the challenging questions. Sometimes those questions don't even need to be answered, just asked. Respect and trust become the cornerstones of the relationship. When we get to the point of not feeling the need to one-up each other with stories and accomplishments, we are free to enjoy a relationship where giving is more rewarding than taking.

Case in point: Paula was asked to be a guest lecturer for an executive graduate program in the School of Public Health at our alma mater, the University of North Carolina at Chapel Hill. In the audience was a staff member, Don, who was in our industry and a mutual contact. Her talk piqued his interest, and he sought her out to ask about her views as a woman in the industry. Men often seek out the female perspective, even if it is not always adequately represented in C-suites and boards of directors.

Shortly thereafter, Don asked Paula to suggest some women who might be qualified to serve on a for-profit board of a growing company where he was the chair. She gladly put forth names for a position that many working women aspire to — paid board work. What she didn't know was that Don had also asked me for some suggestions. I suggested Paula. We were both happy to help other women achieve this success. I could not be more thrilled that Paula now sits on this board sharing her expertise and strategic insight.

Conversely, Paula was more than willing to help me when I asked her to be a reference. Paula spoke with the chair of the board, and in Paula's words, "I provided a glowing reference for Lisa to join as CEO." Give and take. Support and complement. It's a beautiful thing.

There is true joy and fulfillment to be found in helping others, whether it is feeding the hungry or helping a peer achieve professional success. If we are comfortable in our own skin, we are able — even eager — to complement one another and not feel the need to constantly compete. Except on Fitbit. We still compete on Fitbit. But we consider that "healthy" competition, so it's all good.

Dear Cynthia,

You've come a long way from a difficult childhood, moving all the time, living in public housing and never quite feeling accepted. By being determined and resilient you have overcome those obstacles and achieved more than you dreamed. The path ahead of you is full of even more opportunity and success, if you continue to be brave and honest and work hard. Building a meaningful career is not easy, but remember these three things. First, your character is the foundation that your career is built upon. Second, the relationships you develop will ultimately bring the greatest meaning and joy to your career. And third, your ability to reason, analyze and ask thoughtful questions will be the mortar that keeps it all together.

Being honest with yourself and living a life of integrity are the underpinnings of your own character. Ethical people are the building blocks of great companies that serve their clients and their communities. Cutting corners on truthfulness may be tempting, especially when you're afraid of failure or reprisal. You will be upset when you see others do it and seemingly not suffer consequences. But over time, the truth is always revealed, and those who have taken short cuts will see their reputations crumble into dust.

Even though you are very self-sufficient, you have already seen that you need others to help you achieve your goals. With people around you working towards a common goal, together you can move mountains if you believe in each other. Never assume you are the smartest person in the room. You can learn something from everyone. As a leader, you have an innate ability to care deeply about each member of your team. Work hard to ensure they can be as successful as possible and create an environment of camaraderie. After all, isn't that what you want from your leader?

Business is about problem solving. Your natural ability to analyze and solve problems only gets better when you share your ideas and listen to others. Ask the tough questions, and be willing to answer them. Together you will develop the best solutions for all the stakeholders.

These guiding principles will help you stay grounded as you experiment with building a lifelong body of work. But whether your experiments succeed or fail, what is most important is learning from each trial. Every relationship and every event in life has at least one nugget of wisdom to be found. Search for it and expect to see it. Keeping a sense of hopefulness and positive forward movement will take courage in your darkest hours. But I know you can do it. Continue to work hard and be humble and also be brave!

Much love,
Cynthia

Cynthia A. Williams
Chief Corporate Communications Officer and Senior Executive VP
Retired, BB&T

8

Adversity Builds Character

"It's not whether you get knocked down, it's whether you get up."
~ Vince Lombardi

by Lisa

Fall 2008. New York City. It was a heady time in my career. I was the CEO of a healthcare technology start-up company, and we were about to make a big splash. After working for months to secure a major international round of funding, we landed a pre-eminent venture capitalist to take the lead. I flew to New York City with my CFO to announce the deal to the world. We inked all the paperwork after 5 p.m., so the money would be wired the next morning. That night our team celebrated victory with dinner at The Kimberly Hotel in Midtown Manhattan. The next day we would make all the rounds — a full day of interviews with investors, analysts and journalists. Mission accomplished!

Or so I thought.

The U.S market was volatile that season, but nothing prepared me for the phone call I got the next morning at breakfast. It was the manager for our lead investor. The conversation was short and sweet. His words came at me in snippets, as if through a tunnel, but they hit me like a freight train. *Market crashed ... Investor is no longer comfortable with this amount of money ... We're really sorry ... Best of luck ... Wish I had something better to say.*

And just like that, the deal that we thought was going to make us ... vanished. And with it, the company's future. My mind clicked through practical questions. *What am I going to do with my team? What am I going to do about the appointment that starts in an hour?* I forced myself to move quickly — calling my chairman, my CFO, the PR agency that would need to cancel the interviews. I packed my bags and headed back to the office, knowing there would be dark days ahead.

On September 29, 2008, the Dow Jones Industrial Average fell 777 points, the largest point drop on any single day, and kicked off a recession that lasted into the next year. I knew in my gut we didn't have the runway to keep the company going without the funding, and in that climate there would be no other investors.

When I got back to North Carolina, I met with my team, I apologized, and I told them I would try to help them find other jobs. In a touching show of solidarity, some of them offered to stay and work for free as we closed the company down. We managed to avoid bankruptcy and pay our bills by packaging and selling some of the company's assets. That was some consolation — but there was no getting around the devastation, the disappointment, the embarrassment I was feeling. I had failed.

I withdrew professionally for a few months to lick my wounds. I could see how easy it would be to fall into a pity party. I could see how this adversity could become a crutch for every bad thing that might happen to me. I realized it could make me bitter … or better.

Define and Refine

It's one thing to pontificate about how failure is an inevitable part of business. And it is. No doubt it is motivating to recount the stories of Abe Lincoln's string of failed political races, Michael Jordan getting cut from his high school basketball team or Walt Disney getting fired from a newspaper because he had no imagination. But it's another thing to live through that failure. It is hard. And it hurts.

Losing this deal was the biggest professional blow to my confidence I had experienced. I knew I would not, could not, let failure define me, but rather would look for the lessons that might refine me. My choices were going to build or tear down my character. My personal brand was certainly put to the test. On my worst day, was I going to resort to hurling blame, insults or even objects at others? (I have had bosses throw things at me in fits of anger. That thought never crossed my mind.) Or was I going to respond rationally and honestly and exhibit control and good judgment? I knew my personal brand was one of integrity and leading by example, so making those choices was not difficult. I just had to remain true to who I was. Even though the chips were down, remembering my personal brand enabled me to keep my head up as I walked out the door.

In terms of lessons learned, I needed to accept the responsibility that was mine but realize I could not carry the weight of the stock market on my shoulders. I needed to let that go. From a practical standpoint, the experience impressed on me the importance of staying current on bills, operating with a cash reserve, and not outspending the company's resources. From a leadership standpoint, it reinforced the need and the value of being transparent with employees in the good times and the bad. It was very difficult to call in my employees and say, "I failed, we failed and we are going to lose our jobs." But there was never a question it was the right thing to do.

What I found is that transparency was actually freeing. It strengthened my relationship with most of the people who were going through the disappointment with me. In fact, even in the midst of the shutdown I had people tell me they would like to work for me again … and some did. One of the original investors recommended me for other jobs and even came back to me years later and offered to invest in another venture in which I was involved. I was blown away and initially pushed back at the idea. This man had lost money with me once; I didn't really want to go there again. So, I was both humbled and flattered when he told me it was the integrity that I exhibited under pressure that he remembered and valued most.

Somehow, when I was feeling my worst, I was also becoming my best.

Growth Opportunities

Adversity comes in many shapes and sizes, yet all provide the opportunity for growth. Paula often shares this story of how a setback with a customer became the catalyst her company needed to change its ways and improve its services:

As head of sales, I was leading a team in a proposal to a major customer that could have been a $25 million deal. I had assembled what I thought was a great team to make the pitch. When we lost the bid and were told it was because we were too arrogant, it was a big blow. Where had we gone wrong?

As it turns out, while we thought our proposal offered in-depth information and knowledge, they thought we were telling them what to do and even questioning their current way of doing things. They viewed us as competing with them instead of complementing them. They did not want to partner with a company they viewed as egotistical. Wow — that was tough to hear. But we listened and then looked inward, deciding we had just given ourselves an example of what not to do. From then on, we crafted our proposals and presentations differently to exhibit our knowledge but not in a way that would threaten or offend the customer. It was a worthwhile lesson. It changed our checks and balances and approval process for the better. Our $25 million setback turned into a growth opportunity for the company that was priceless.

Negative Feedback

We all love giving and receiving a compliment. But negative feedback? Especially if it's personal? That's tough. A common tool used in leadership development is the 360-degree feedback method. The process, in which employees receive confidential, anonymous feedback from the people who work around them (managers, peers, and direct reports), is the gold standard, and Paula and I have both participated in 360 feedback several times — giving and receiving. Our results usually were pretty similar to those of many senior-level women who participate — we were viewed by others as too defensive. For ambitious women, this was hard to hear. We like to think we have poker faces but have found out we really didn't. Yet, we knew there was truth in the perception. We both had to learn to recognize it in order to stop it — easier said than done. Paula took a step back and realized how coming across as defensive in meetings actually ended up being a double whammy against her.

Paula: *When I would behave in a way that was viewed as defensive and was told as much, I would hold onto that and behave differently in the next meeting — but not in the right way. I would be more reserved and not as transparent or bold. It was a vicious cycle: Get defensive — be embarrassed — shut down. It was my way of professionally pouting.*

It took some true self-awareness, which is the key to growth, and a determined effort to move past that. I conditioned myself to stop and think before speaking, to make sure a sharp-tongued response didn't slip out. I learned the words that set people off and avoided them. Instead of saying, "I strongly disagree with that decision," I might say, "Have we considered?" or "A potential solution may be ..." By taking the "I" and "you" out and having evidence ready to support my viewpoints, I turned that negative feedback into something constructive. Although it is always a work in progress.

Just as ignoring negative feedback can hold us back personally and professionally, shying away from giving it when necessary erodes our credibility as a leader. It might be difficult to tell team members something you know they don't want to hear, but consider that a good sign. It means you care enough to give them useful information they need to grow and change. In fact, if you are going to get pleasure out of giving negative feedback you might want to rethink your motive for giving it. If it's to get back, get even or get revenge, don't give it. The goal should always be improvement.

Difficult Relationships

We all have difficult relationships at work that we need to manage. As we have discussed, often the toughest relationships are the ones we have with other women.

Sharon and Paula, both senior leaders, had been adversaries for a long time. There were long-held grudges and perceived betrayals. Eventually, it became clear that letting the relationship fester was not only hurting the company, but holding them both back. Paula knew that if she wanted to maintain her credibility and continue to move forward, she needed to turn things around with Sharon.

Paula: *I invited Sharon to meet in a neutral setting. Over a nice glass of wine, we both took a deep breath and honestly aired our grievances. A surprising thing happened when we let our guards down: I saw insecurity under her hard exterior, which immediately softened me. In a tearful exchange we hashed out our frustrations with one another. It required each of us to accept some blame, apologize, extend forgiveness, and be willing to start again. Which we did.*

Soon afterward, Sharon joined my team, and we focused on working with each other instead of against each other. Male colleagues bet me she wouldn't last a year on my team. They were wrong. I offered her trust and space to grow, and she did not abuse it. Our relationship ended up being good for us and the company because we both grew. She added to her knowledge and skill set (and has since gone on to join the C-suite of another company), and I not only added to my credibility as an effective leader, I got a deep sense of satisfaction from turning a competitive relationship into a productive working relationship. In another testament to Complementing Beats Competing, I can truly say helping Sharon achieve her potential was very rewarding, and it built character for both of us.

Adversity Breeds Innovation

When my right thumb joint started hurting about seven years ago, I thought maybe I was texting too much and just needed to give it a rest. A visit to an orthopedic surgeon revealed there was no cartilage left in my thumb joint and it was covered with bone spurs. My left thumb soon followed. What turned out to be osteoarthritis was painful and getting worse. After I went through several cortisone shots — their own brand of searing pain — adding supplements and being diligent about my diet, my doctor suggested corrective surgery.

After researching the procedure and hearing more than a few "less than positive" stories, I decided that wasn't the answer for me and continued to look for a solution that would relieve the pain. The more I read about stem cell therapy in larger joints, the more I wondered whether my own stem cells could help my condition. Transplants in such small joints had not been done before, and it took me a while to find a doctor willing to try. OK, I had to beg.

But once I signed all the experimental release forms, it was a go. After a 90-minute procedure, two months with immobilizing braces on my hands and arms and several more months of hand therapy, I finally experienced some relief. My thumbs are not perfect, but they are significantly better. The old saying "no pain, no gain" is definitely true.

There were silver linings. My doctor has since performed this treatment on others and presented it to colleagues as a viable experimental option. Personally, this painful journey revealed to me an incredible support network I could not have imagined. I was so used to being the one in charge that when I was forced to sit still, amazing things happened. Friends and family became my hands — cooking meals, feeding me, sitting with me, bringing me flowers. It was not only humbling, but it taught me a lot about gratitude and empathy. It made me more aware of how even the tiniest things matter. It also gave me much needed time to reflect on and appreciate the many blessings in my life.

A Gift to be Shared

We have found that one of the biggest gifts that comes from adversity is not just what we learn but the lessons we are able to share. Wisdom that is hoarded helps no one. We can't give tips on how to live a life devoid of adversity. We are most stretched and strengthened by going through the experience ourselves. But we can help one another by sharing our stories and how we deal with life's difficulties.

We can both tell you we wish we had embraced adversity sooner. The longer you wait, the more awkward things become and the harder it is to move forward. I wish I had jumped back into the workforce sooner after I shut down the company. Paula wishes she and Sharon had worked things out earlier. The quicker we deal with adversity, the less time and space we give to negativity and the sooner we can make positive changes. We live, learn and, we hope, come away with more knowledge and a greater confidence to tackle the next thing.

> "Every problem has a gift for you in its hands."
> — Richard Bach

When we learn from our mistakes, when we make the best of a bad situation, when we turn a sour relationship around, when new ideas and procedures emerge from dark, painful places, adversity has given us a gift. The gift is the hope for something better, the reward that flows from honesty and integrity, the fulfillment that comes from sharing what we have learned and the peace that comes when we make choices that affirm who we are.

Dear Tashni-Ann,

You are phenomenal.

Those lil' dreams of yours are admirable, but you are capable of leaving a greater impact on anything you pursue in life. Dream bigger, Tash. Dream bigger.

You are wired to pursue perfection in all that you do. Anything less than an 'A' on an assignment or a performance below your self-imposed standards is unacceptable to you. However, I want you to understand that the pursuit of happiness is riddled with opportunities to create memories wrapped in pure joy. Do not be so immersed in hard work and studying that you miss valuable lessons in building longstanding friendships, smelling the roses and living in the moment.

There are valuable lessons in this life that aren't taught through assignments, but they are the parts of life that will cultivate your resilience and grit – both of which will help you to navigate tough times at work and at home. The most important thing you can do to prepare yourself for this beautiful, Divinely orchestrated life of yours is to understand that experiences, not accolades, are what will make your life rewarding for you, and a model for others. Be patient, relax a tad and enjoy all that you are doing as learning experiences, and not goals to be conquered.

Years from now, all of the dreams that you will be living will be nothing like you imagine today. Your job, your personal life, your ambition – all will be constructed around people and ideas who you don't even know exist.

You may think now that tears are symptoms of weakness. But actually they are signs of strength. And when you find that strength is best fortified in the comfort of assuring words or support from friends and family, the better equipped you will be to see opportunities instead of obstacles.

So life's disappointments yet to come will not derail you. They will empower you because you know that you are strong enough to remain diligent in the face of adversity.

Years from now you will find true happiness because you learned to master perspective and resilience. And these things – not money or accolades – will make you richer than you ever imagined.

Lastly, pack a winter coat. You're headed to America!

Tashni-Ann

Tashni-Ann Dubroy, Ph.D.
Executive VP and COO, Howard University
Former President, Shaw University

Whom Can I Serve Today?

"Don't chase success. Instead, decide to make a difference and success will find you."

~ Jon Gordon

by Paula

Little Granny has been one of my favorite people in the whole world. Although I was one of six grandchildren, my mother's mother always made me feel special, whether it was on long shell-seeking walks on the beach or on trips to Boylan-Pearce department store on Saturday afternoons for a little high-fashion shoe shopping. My personal brand includes being a server, in large part, from working with and watching Little Granny run the family restaurant for 40 years.

As one of nine children growing up on a tobacco farm, Little Granny was well-accustomed to hard work. And even at just five feet tall, she had a way of making her presence known. She ran the register at the restaurant, took care of customers, and called everyone by name — with a smile. Everyone loved "Miss Baxley." She was genteel and kind, but firm when she needed to be. When she caught people trying to steal food, her response was always the same: *"If you had just asked me I would have given it to you."* I learned so much from Little Granny, and not only about working hard and serving others with kindness. As it turns out, it was she who added real purpose and meaning to my professional life.

In 1995, a new type 2 diabetes drug was launched in the United States. As the outsourced project manager for its development, I worked for four years with a multinational pharmaceutical company conducting clinical trials up to its eventual FDA approval. It wasn't until I was home with my newborn daughter a month after launch that those years' work took on a new and important meaning.

Little Granny had been diagnosed with type 2 diabetes in the 1980s and had controlled it with diet, daily monitoring, and oral drugs. But when she came to visit her new great-granddaughter that day, she told me the drug was no longer working and her doctor had told her it was time to begin taking insulin shots. When she asked her doctor about trying this new product, he said no. *"It's too new. We don't know enough about it,"* he warned. Well, I knew a lot about it, and I wasn't going to let Little Granny experience a serious downgrade in her quality of life without more investigation.

I called the president of the pharmaceutical company at home. She was a highly intelligent physician who had been the lead drug developer, and I admired her greatly and valued her opinion. After discussing my grandmother's case, she said there was no reason she shouldn't be on the new oral drug; in fact, Little Granny was exactly the kind of patient it was designed to help. Little Granny went back and told her doctor she was going on the new drug, and that was that. For 20 more years, Granny enjoyed the benefits of the drug and improved her quality of life before she eventually went on insulin. My family and I enjoyed 20 more Thanksgiving and Christmas meals with her at the table, sharing the love of food and family.

I often tell people that was when I went from having a job to having a career I was passionate about. That I could relate my work to an impact like that in the life of someone I love made a significant impression on me. Having a feeling of fulfillment doesn't begin to describe it. All of the data, all of the analyses, all of the testing — it now wore the face of my grandmother. Before, I might have thought the success of a new drug was simply a vehicle to get the next promotion, more credibility with customers, and a lucrative contract for the company. Yes, all of those things happened. But what gave me passion and purpose in my work was not the money — it was about giving hope and changing lives. I suppose I knew this in an abstract way — after all, it was in our marketing material — but watching *my* work improve Little Granny's life really hit home. I discovered how I could use my work to achieve my purpose. I realized my path was to stay at one company and work in a variety of roles that would not only challenge me and support my family but bring life-changing drugs to market.

This was my place to make a greater impact. It meant I was working for more than a paycheck, and that is when I began to experience true fulfillment through my work. This wasn't always the case for me or for most women of my generation. The idea of experiencing real fulfillment in your work wasn't expected or even considered important — but that is quickly changing.

Millennials are demanding work that is both flexible and meaningful; they expect purpose. Corporate Social Responsibility (CSR) has become an integral part of the global corporate culture, so there are more opportunities than ever to find work you can feel good about. Companies engaged in CSR — that is, improving society — gave more than 18 billion dollars to charities in 2016. A Cone Communications Employee Engagement Study recently found that two-thirds of millennials would not work for a company that does not have strong CSR commitments, and 83 percent would be more loyal if they felt they could improve society at work.

It's refreshing to see that business sense has caught up with common sense. Living and working with purpose correlate to our personal happiness, which, in turn, leads to greater corporate success. And did we mention that companies with women in leadership roles (board members or executives) had higher levels of CSR engagement than those without? It's a fact.

The Gift that Keeps on Giving

86,400 seconds. That's how much time you and I and everyone else have in a day. No more. No less. How will I use them? Whom can I help today? Do I *have time* to help others, or will I *make time*? Over the course of her career, these are the questions Lisa increasingly asked herself. They led her on a journey toward volunteerism outside the workplace that found her doing everything from chairing a gala for a local non-profit to helping a friend throw a launch party for her new book. She decided that using her business skills to help non-profits be more effective is one of the most fulfilling ways she can use some of those 86,400 seconds.

> **Lisa:** *I'm at my best when I'm helping somebody. It's that simple. It took me a while to realize that's how I am hard-wired, but it has opened up a whole new world of possibilities. There are so many fantastic organizations out there operating on shoestring budgets that can benefit from skill sets that are commonplace in the*

corporate world, whether it is organizational structure, maintaining functional donor databases, or marketing and messaging. I love to help fill those gaps and make connections that help others achieve their goals. That's why my relationship with Peggy has been so rewarding.

Peggy and I became friends when our children were in kindergarten, and we immediately hit it off. We were both professional moms in the health sciences industry, and we both used our faith as a compass. We just clicked. For years, I have admired Peggy as I watched her work multiple jobs, raise two children and still make time for giving back.

Spending time with her inspires me to be a better person. As her dad struggled with lung cancer, her family lived his bucket list with him and made priceless memories before he passed away. Motivated to give that same opportunity to others, Peggy took a bold step and started the Fill Your Bucket List Foundation. It's similar to the Make-A-Wish Foundation, except that it's for adults who live below the poverty line. In three years, the foundation has filled more than three dozen wishes, including providing a first-ever family vacation for a dying mother and her children and sending a 19-year-old brain cancer patient to see Niagara Falls. It has been a privilege to serve with Peggy to help fund these cancer patients' wishes and provide their families with once-in-a-lifetime memories.

Of course, I have also found joy in giving back for something as simple as putting an aspiring young artist looking for exposure in touch with a local nonprofit looking for art for a big fundraiser. Whether it is in the community, at school or at church, there are endless opportunities out there to make a big impact in someone's life IF you take the time to notice them. Many times I didn't notice because my calendar was so jammed. It is easy to get carried away with all the things on your to-do list. And certainly, there are seasons of our lives where we have more or less time to share than others. As I have said, there was a time in my life when volunteering was a plastic ball. Now it's a glass ball.

Even so, I've learned the importance of setting boundaries on my time (remember, we are not Superwomen). I have said "no" to some things so I could say "yes" to others. In fact, I originally had to tell Peggy I could not serve on her board because my schedule was too full, but when other things moved off my plate, I was able to get more involved with her foundation. Ultimately, I found if I allowed myself to be spread so thin that I did not have any time to give back, my emotional tank wasn't quite full. For me to feel my best, giving back had to be a priority. Peggy encourages people to covet their calendar and schedule giving back just as you would sleep and exercise. She has experienced, as have I, that when giving back is made a priority, your own priorities take on a profound clarity.

"It has made my life richer and puts priorities in place quickly," Peggy explains. "Seeing the face and the strength of the patients really helps me focus on what's important. It also forces me to not sweat the small stuff."

One of the coolest things about giving back is becoming part of the circle of giving. When I connect with others, opportunities open up for more giving, and collectively we can accomplish even greater things. The Fill Your Bucket List Foundation's first wish was *given to Ylonda, a mother of three who was battling breast cancer and who had never been able to afford a family vacation. Peggy's family sacrificed their own summer vacation so they could fund that first wish — a Disney cruise for Ylonda's family. They made great memories, which became even more treasured when Ylonda died six months later. But the story didn't end there. Ylonda's sister and children were so touched by the generosity of the fledgling foundation, they started selling t-shirts and sent Peggy a check for $1,400 to be used for the next patient's wish. Wow! Giving is truly the gift that keeps on giving, and I love being a part of that circle. It provides me joy and a feeling of contentment and purpose I don't find anywhere else.*

If you want to feel a fullness that is off the charts, get your children involved in giving back. You might start small when they are young, shopping for gifts or groceries together for those in need. When they are a little older they can help stuff envelopes for a non-profit (Peggy's children have been involved in the work of the foundation since day one), or set up tables and chairs for an event. Then one day, when you least expect it, your child might come to you on a cold winter day and ask to take blankets and gloves to pass out to the homeless downtown. Then they might choose to go again and take their friends with them. And then they might go out into the world and make their own mark by working to improve the lives of others. Watching my own children do this has reminded me that whether we realize it or not, our priorities and choices become our legacy. When we help others, it's not just the recipient and giver who receive. I've seen how it encourages others who are watching, like our children, to want to join the circle of giving.

So, whom can you serve today?

Mentor Other Women

Lisa and I have a shared vision, and a shared lament. It is one of the main reasons we teamed up to write this book. We believe women need to be helping other women achieve their professional potential in meaningful ways. And we believe one of the best ways to do that is through mentoring. Neither of us had much of that while we were coming up through the ranks, but looking back, oh, how we wish we had. We wish we had asked another woman to be our mentor or that another woman had offered to mentor us. And we wish someone had told us that it was OK to ask for help and advice — that it wouldn't make us look weak. In fact, a mentor might have clued us in on some of the nuances we missed in our work relationships and made our paths a bit less bumpy. If someone we trusted had told us there might be a better way to get from point A to point B besides a hard-driving straight line, we might have made deeper connections sooner. We are fortunate to have found each other and to be forging this new path together, one we hope will lead to a greater good.

I am especially proud of my founding involvement with the Women Inspired Network (WIN) at my former company, which fosters a corporate culture that inspires women to be leaders and facilitates mentoring at all levels. Seven years later the group boasted more than 1,500 members worldwide, with more than a dozen chapters from Kansas to South Africa. When the organization won the Healthcare Businesswoman Association's ACE Award for efforts to strengthen the advancement, commitment and engagement of women's careers in the healthcare industry, it was both humbling and gratifying. I did not set out to create such a thing, but I knew women needed advocacy and support in their careers. As is often the case, once a resonating idea is birthed, it takes on a life of its own. Those same ideas can be applied across all industries.

Some mentoring relationships are more formal and involve bi-weekly, monthly, or quarterly meetups, while others transition into simply receiving texts, emails or phone calls when there's a need. Regardless, it is an investment of time but one we find immensely satisfying.

Lisa: *When I met Sara I could tell right away that she was smart, but I could also see she was insecure and unsure of herself, a common plight for women caught in the Confidence Gap. She needed a career change but didn't know where or how to move on. My goal was to help her solidify and articulate her personal brand and hone her skill set. I don't like telling mentees what to do; instead I ask them questions I hope will lead them to answers, or I suggest reading books or articles I think will help put them on the right path. We usually talk about our Venn diagram — What are you good at? What are you passionate about? What can you make money doing? — and then look for the points of intersection.*

Over the course of five or six years, I worked with Sara on everything from developing her own voice — and doing so with confidence and authority — to interviewing, negotiating a salary, and considering how she could use her skills inside and outside her company. When the time came, I was happy to help her get a job interview with someone in my network. I can't tell you how many times the president of that company has come back to me to thank me for sending her his way. Watching her grow in her career, become more sure of herself, and become a leader just makes me smile. The fact that she now shares her talents with other women is a bonus. It's like watching a pebble put out ripples in the water … and who knows where it will end? That's what we can do for one another.

We encourage every woman to have at least one mentor, maybe more, someone above you who is willing to invest the time, help you navigate your path, find your strengths, and point out areas to improve. Some things to keep in mind when choosing a mentor:

- Find someone you trust. Listen to your gut. What is her reputation? Listen to how she speaks about others.
- Look for someone who has a path you respect or admire. How has she handled successes and challenges?
- While not absolutely necessary, consider a mentor in a similar field/industry. Don't ask your boss.
- Be open to a co-mentor relationship with someone in a non-competing industry. Lisa and I act as co-mentors to each other, and it works.

Some companies offer to match people in mentoring programs; others even train people to become mentors. Whether you are helping another woman advance her career or receiving valuable insights from a woman who has walked the path before you, the experience will transform and reward you.

Kindness Connects Us

I was a Daddy's girl, no doubt about it. As the third daughter before my brother came along, I was the tomboy, hanging out and going to ball games with him, and keeping score for his Civitan softball team. Dad taught me about sales and had the best network of anyone I knew. Achieving success in my career meant even more to me because I knew it made him proud.

Watching Dad suffer from multiple myeloma the last three and a half years of his life was especially difficult for me. I still remember that Monday in April, sitting in our morning meeting at work and being distracted. I couldn't stop thinking about Dad. On the spur of the moment, I grabbed my bag and went to have lunch with him and Mom at my childhood home. He didn't look good, and I didn't want to leave. It was completely against my nature and overdeveloped sense of corporate responsibility, but something told me not to go back to the office that day. I sat with Dad, talking and welcoming the visitors that were never in short supply for him. There were "I love you's" and tears, and at 4:30 that afternoon he took his last breath … and I was heartbroken.

I share this story not to re-live the sadness but to offer an insight and explain the impact of what happened next. The insight is, listen to your gut. Work responsibilities are important, no doubt, and should not be blown off lightly, but a woman's intuition should not be ignored either. Don't be afraid to listen to that little voice inside you and take action. The unexpected impact of my father's death was a deluge of kindness, like I have never before experienced, enveloping me. Hundreds of people came to express their sympathies in a standing-room-only service. People I hadn't seen in years and professional acquaintances, many of whom I was not close to, tracked down my home address and sent flowers and cards, the kindest of notes, and Bible verses. They shared personal stories of love and loss and showed me a side of themselves I had never seen. It was unexpected and touching beyond measure.

I have kept every one of those cards. They brought me such comfort and made me feel loved at a very difficult time. The cards automatically connected me to people on a deeper level, and we all long to feel connected.

Sometimes you don't realize the importance or strength of connections until times of crisis. I know I didn't. Dad taught me a lot during his life and, as it turns out, in his death too. I learned that kindness is more than a nice thing to do. Kindness connects us. Kindness changes lives. Every time we extend a kindness to someone or someone extends a kindness to us, a connection is made, our lives are changed and a sense of purpose and fulfillment fill a space inside us we may not have realized even existed.

In business, we hear the phrase, "It's all about relationships." That's true, but we would also add, "It's all about kindness." And that's something that is within everyone's reach because it doesn't matter how big or small the kindness is, it isn't based on salaries or titles. It could be a compliment or a smile or a quick handwritten note of encouragement that will brighten someone's day.

As a successful professional, don't be afraid to step out and challenge yourself to use your goal-oriented nature to accomplish something worthwhile, something that is not self-serving, but something that connects … something that elevates … something that is kind.

Go ahead. Take the risk. Make the connection. Share your talents. Be kind. And above all, *Remember Who You Are.*

Dear Susan,

I know you are grieving the loss of your college roommate, Marilyn. Her death from breast cancer at such a young age and with two small children is indeed tragic. Experience tells me that the grief will never leave you entirely, but it will come and go, and it will lighten. Grief can also transform into an extraordinary energy that can propel you to give back in the world.

You are doing well at 36, young one, even if you feel unsettled. It is natural for you to wonder whether you should stay in your field, go back for more education, consider moving to a larger city, or all of these. It is normal to question how important your work in the world really is and whether it is personally meaningful. And now you are also wondering whether you can make a difference in cancer – so that young children don't have to lose their mother. I believe that you can, and that these goals are not mutually exclusive. You can do well by doing good, and you can do that in many fields and in any geography.

Giving back to the world, to society, and to individuals is a noble goal. It will bring you a lot of satisfaction, but it will also bring you heartache. When you work with medical or social ills, and try to improve and save lives, there are always failures. It is part of the territory. A challenge for you is to use those failures as impetus to work harder and do more. Doing this work will also bring you joy beyond your imagination. I remember the first time a neighbor came to me with a small gift and said, with tears in his eyes, that he was convinced that I saved his life by connecting him to the right doctor doing novel research that worked for him. I still feel pleased and also humble when I think of that.

Young one, if you start to waver in your conviction, remember why you chose to give back. What made you KNOW this is what you must do. When you're a lot older, what you will remember is the good you've been able to create. You'll think back on those times and those people with an incredible warmth and be able to reflect on the good you've provided in the world, on what you've given back. Large or small. It will exceed any award you've received or any promotion you've earned. It is universal, and it is eternal.

With love,
Susan

Susan Braun
CEO
The V Foundation for Cancer Research

Be You

It's the connections we make with others and for others that will bring us the success, balance and fulfillment we desire as real, yet imperfect, women. Even those with high-powered careers need one another on a genuine and transparent level. When you see that woman who appears to be "the whole package," remember, she is not so unlike you. Great heights are attainable for you, too, not by being her, but by Remembering Who YOU Are. By being other people's missing pieces and offering vulnerability through shared experiences, we can inspire confidence in one another that will help all of us achieve our greatest potential.

Every day we see firsthand that if you pursue meaning and purpose, success seems to find you. We would not have thought it when we were 30 years old, but we do now. Many of our peers who have shared their letters with you agree. There are so many lessons to learn and so many ways to give back, whether through mentoring, volunteering, or even offering a smile of encouragement. The key is to take action.

We hope you will join us in embracing one another's successes and learning from each other's experiences by sharing your story. Let's keep the conversation going! Visit us at www.habergeon.com.

Acknowledgments

There are so many wonderful friends and associates who've helped us throughout our careers and in the writing of *Remember Who You Are* that we could fill several pages, so let us first say thanks to everyone whose support has brought this book to life.

Without Jennifer Buehrle Williams, there wouldn't be a book. You have a way with words. You captured who we are as you put pen to paper. You were able to help organize our thoughts and meld our voices — and to capture parts of our stories we might otherwise not have remembered ourselves. Always inquisitive and truly able to articulate stories in a fascinating way, we appreciate your journalistic skills.

Eric Frederick, as we told you — you made the book better with your editing prowess. Need we say more? You taught us journalism 101 as you painstakingly showed us the 'why' behind each of your recommendations.

A special thanks to dear friends Debbie W. Wilson, Peggy Gibson Carroll and Debra Morgan, for enhancing our lives and for allowing parts of your stories to be incorporated here. You tirelessly pour your lives into others, and we are better because of you.

What can we say about the forewords and letters? Gail, Bob, Laurie, Shideh, Heidi, Jenn, Iris, Louise, Cynthia, Tashni, and Susan, you rock! Each of you made this a stronger book in your own personal and unique way. The wisdom you shared with your younger selves and our readers — in a transparent way — shows us how real powerhouse women (and men) like you achieved the trifecta. Your words enriched us, and we know they will inspire others too. We appreciate the time it took to reflect, dig deep and then reveal.

In 2002, Alan Boyd encouraged the two of us to meet for lunch. You predicted we would become fast friends — and you were so right!

Jim and Chris Howard, and the team at Morgan James, from the beginning you believed in us. Thank you for your guidance along this journey. And a shout out to the team at Marbles Kids Museum, especially April.

Thanks to our moms, Amy and Barbara, for showing us strength, giving us the drive to be independent and the courage to better ourselves.

A special thank you goes to our husbands, Greg and Ed, whose faithful support and encouragement over the past three decades has put wind in our sails. You helped us to achieve balance. You bless us in many ways. We love you both!

And finally, we appreciate you, our readers, colleagues and those we've coached or mentored.

Notes

INTRODUCTION: THE MISSING PIECE

1. Upspeak. Lebowitz, Shana. "How 2 Common Speech Quirks Can Destroy Your Reputation at Work." *Business Insider*, Business Insider, 3 Aug. 2015, www.businessinsider.com/upspeak-vocal-fry-hurt-your-reputation-2015-7.

CHAPTER ONE: BUILDING YOUR BRAND

1. Power poses. Amy Cuddy, Ph.D., *Presence: Bringing Your Boldest Self to your Biggest Challenges*. (New York: Little, Brown and Company, 2015).

2. Digital footprint. Dorie Clark, "How to Protect Your Online Reputation," January 15, 2015. www.forbes.com/sites/dorieclark/2015/01/15/how-to-protect-your-online-reputation/#2cbc6acc5e19.

3. Attractiveness. Jaclyn S. Wong, University of Chicago, Andrew M. Penner, University of California-Irvine, "Gender and the Returns to Attractiveness," *Research in Social Stratification and Mobility*, Volume 44, (June 2016): 113–123.

CHAPTER TWO: DELIVERING X PLUS

1. Grit. Angela Duckworth, Ph.D. Grit: *The Power of Passion and Perseverance.* (New York: Scribner, 2016).

CHAPTER THREE: AUTHENTIC LEADERSHIP

1. Level 5 Leadership. Jim Collins, *Good to Great: Why Some Companies Make the Leap … and Others Don't.* (New York: Harper Business, 2001).

2. Humility. Salib, Jeanine PrimeElizabeth. "The Best Leaders Are Humble Leaders." *Harvard Business Review*, 1 Nov. 2014, hbr.org/2014/05/the-best-leaders-are-humble-leaders.

3. Humility. Research brief. "Humility is a key to high performance and effective leadership," Michael G. Foster School of Business, University of Washington. September 19, 2012. http://foster.uw.edu/research-brief/humility-is-a-key-to-high-performance-and-effective-leadership.

4. Confidence. Katty Kay and Claire Shipman, "Closing the Confidence Gap," *The Atlantic.* May 2014.

5. Growth mindset. Carol S. Dweck, Ph.D., *Mindset: The New Psychology of Success.* (New York: Ballentine Books, 2016).

6. Lean in. Sheryl Sandberg and Nell Scovell, *Lean In: Women, Work and the Will to Lead.* (New York: Alfred A. Knopf. 2013).

7. Women in meetings. Kathryn Heath, Jill Flynn and Mary Davis Holt, "Women, Find Your Voice," *Harvard Business Review.* June 2014.

8. Be bold but not bully. Jim Rohn, *Leading an Inspired Life.* (Illinois: Nightingale-Conant Corp. 1996).

CHAPTER FIVE: CALENDAR JAM

1. Over-scheduled children. Alvin Rosenfeld, MD and Nicole Wise, *The Over-Scheduled Child: Avoiding the Hyper-Parenting Trap.* (New York: St. Martin's Press, 2000).

2. Texting. Susan Weinschenk, Ph.D., "Why We're All Addicted to Texts, Twitter, and Google," *Psychology Today.* September 11, 2012.

CHAPTER SIX: CONQUERING GUILT AND WORRY

1. False guilt. Debbie Wilson. *Give Yourself a Break.* (Independent Publishing Platform, 2014).

2. Refocus. Philippians 4: 6-7, New International Version.

3. Guilt all the time. Blair Thill, "Why Women Need To Stop Feeling Guilty About Literally Everything," Elite Daily. http://elitedaily.com/women/think-thin/1471704/index.html.

4. Speaking up. Sheryl Sandberg and Nell Scovell. *Lean In: Women, Work and the Will to Lead.* (New York: Alfred A. Knopf. 2013).

5. Having it all. Anne-Marie Slaughter, "Why Women Still Can't Have It All," *The Atlantic.* July/August 2012.

6. Working mothers. Harvard Business School, "Having A Working Mother Is Good For You," May 18, 2015. http://www.hbs.edu/news/releases/Pages/having-working-mother.aspx.

CHAPTER SEVEN: COMPLEMENTING BEATS COMPETING

1. Female competition. Tracy Vaillancourt, Ph.D., "Do human females use indirect aggression as an intersexual competition strategy?" *Philosophical Transactions Of The Royal Society B: Biological Sciences.* October 28, 2013.
2. Board quotas. Alison Smale and Claire Cain Miller, "Germany Sets Gender Quota in Boardrooms," *The New York Times.* March 6, 2015.
3. Women on Boards. Claire Cain Miller, "Women on the Board: Quotas Have Limited Success," *The New York Times.* June 19, 2014.
4. Gender diversity. 2016 Gender Diversity Index Key Findings. 2020 Women On Boards. 2016. https://www.2020wob.com/companies/2020-gender-diversity-index.
5. Women on Boards. "Why Diversity Matters," *Catalyst.* July 2013.

CHAPTER NINE: WHOM CAN I SERVE TODAY?

1. Corporate social responsibility. 2016 Cone Communications Employee Engagement Study. *Cone Communications.*
2. Corporate giving. Giving USA 2017, The Annual Report on Philanthropy. Giving Statistics. *Charity Navigator.*

About the Authors

Paula Brown Stafford is a clinical research expert, business leader, and lecturer. She is a distinguished alumna at the University of North Carolina at Chapel Hill, where she is also an Adjunct Professor. Previously she was president of clinical development at QuintilesIMS, a Fortune 500 company. She lives in Chapel Hill, NC with her husband and has two adult children.

Lisa T. Grimes is a business leader, coach and speaker. She has spent most of the last 30 years in healthcare and lifestyle start-ups where she has served as CEO of PurThread Technologies, InSite Clinical Trials and AcSentient. She loves to connect people and often does so through her work with non-profit organizations. She lives in Cary, NC with her husband and has two adult sons.

Together, Paula and Lisa founded Habergeon (www.habergeon.com) to help women achieve success, create balance, and experience fulfillment. They are dedicated to giving back and are donating a portion of all proceeds from book sales to some of their favorite charities.

Visit our website:
www.habergeon.com

Morgan James
Speakers Group

www.TheMorganJamesSpeakersGroup.com

We connect Morgan James published authors with live and online events and audiences who will benefit from their expertise.

9 781683 506478